REJECTING
THE DA VINCI CODE

REJECTING
THE DA VINCI CODE

*How a Blasphemous Novel
Brutally Attacks
Our Lord and the Catholic Church*

by

TFP Committee on American Issues

THE AMERICAN SOCIETY FOR THE DEFENSE
OF TRADITION, FAMILY AND PROPERTY — TFP

SPRING GROVE, PENN. 17362

Cover illustration: Painting by Carl Bloch in St. Nicholas Church in Holbaek, Denmark

Dedication page illustration: Statue of the Immaculate Conception in the Piazza di Spagna, Rome.

Copyright © 2005 The American Society for the Defense of Tradition, Family and Property®—TFP®
1358 Jefferson Road, Spring Grove, Penn. 17362–(866) 661-0272
www.tfp.org

All rights reserved. No part of this publication may be reproduced, stored in a retrieval system, or transmitted, in any form or by any means, electronic or mechanical, including photocopying, recording or any information storage and retrieval system, without prior written permission from The American Society for the Defense of Tradition, Family and Property®—TFP®

This book is being distributed as part of the TFP's America Needs Fatima campaign.

The American Society for the Defense of Tradition, Family and Property®, TFP® and America Needs Fatima® are registered names of The Foundation for a Christian Civilization, Inc., a 501(c)(3) tax-exempt organization.

ISBN-13:   978-1-877905-34-6
ISBN-10:   1-877905-34-8
Library of Congress Control Number: 2005933168

Printed in Canada

American TFF Archive

This book is dedicated to the Immaculate Conception, patroness of the United States. We implore her to hasten the triumph of her Immaculate Heart promised at Fatima.

Acknowledgments

The publication of this book was made possible through the generosity of the TFP-America Needs Fatima *Protectors of the Faith* donors listed below:

Distinguished Members
George and Theresa Marie Chouquette

Honored Members
Mrs. Dorothy Pongracz

Special Members
Mr. and Mrs. Christopher Pierce
Miss Yvonne B. Werth

Members
Mrs. Clara Allen
Mrs. Lorene Arko
Mr. Gerald J. Contos
Mr. Matthew E. Konopka
Mrs. Therese Langenberg
Mr. Anthony Lomangino
Mr. Frank J. Palermo
Mr. Thomas Pardo
Mr. and Mrs. Edward Ritchie
Mr. and Mrs. Richard W. Segerstrom and family
Doug and Julie Woodard
Mrs. Lawrence Zimmerer

"About two thousand years ago there appeared in Judea a truly incomparable Personage. By His doctrine He eclipsed all wise men, all miracle workers by His prodigies, all prophets by His prophecies, all saints by His heroism, and all earthly potentates by His power.

"The drama of His life cast the most pathetic tragedies into the shade. His cradle was surrounded by marvels. Then the Child disappeared from view. Thirty years later He came forth from a small out-of-the-way town hidden in the mountains, and cast around Him so great a splendor, as to attract the whole attention of the nation to Himself for three years. The people sought to make Him their king, but their leaders, envying His glory, condemned Him to death and inflicted on Him the ignominy of the crucifixion. But on the third day He rose gloriously from the tomb, and not long after He returned to heaven whence He had come. And thence, notwithstanding the most formidable and oft-repeated opposition, He has made the whole world His kingdom, subjecting nations and monarchs to His yoke.

"This Personage, immeasurably excelling all the heroes whose names and deeds are recorded by history, is He whom we call Our Lord Jesus Christ."

(Fr. Augustine Berthe, C.S.S.R., *Jesus Christ, His Life, His Passion, His Triumph* [St. Louis, Mo.: B. Herder Book Co., 1919], p. iii.)

&) Contents &)

ᛒ PART III ᛓ
The Code Behind the Code
Gnosticism: Doctrine and History

ᛒ BOXES ᛓ

NOTE TO THE READER
Copyright Permission Denied

In the "Frequently Asked Questions" page of his official web site, Dan Brown says he wrote *The Da Vinci Code* with the hope it would stimulate discussion of the faith:

> These authors and I obviously disagree, but the debate that is being generated is a positive powerful force.... Religion has only one true enemy—apathy—and passionate debate is a superb antidote.[1]

Joining the debate, we submitted a request to quote approximately 1,175 words from *The Da Vinci Code* in our book. However, by letter dated August 22, 2005, Brown's publisher, Random House, Inc., denied us copyright permission.

We have accordingly cut back on the use of quotes from *The Da Vinci Code* and apologize to the reader for not being able to present more proof for our case.

It appears that Random House disagrees with Brown and would rather silence debate.

* ᛫ *

References to or quotes from persons, organizations, institutions or publications do not necessarily mean that we agree with their philosophical or religious positions. We adhere firmly to the Catholic Faith and morals and the *philosophia perennis*, especially in its Thomistic expression.

* * *

For documentation purposes, we reference some web sites and publications with objectionable content and, therefore, feel obliged to warn the reader.

---

1. www.danbrown.com/novels/davinci_code/faqs.html.

FOREWORD
by Rev. Fr. Andrew Apostoli, C.F.R.

In the last twenty years we have witnessed an amazing increase of literature that claims to present factual evidence that contradicts or distorts long-standing historical facts or accepted values. This is particularly true in the area of religion, especially regarding the teachings of the Catholic Church. But these "new truths" are almost always nothing more than figments of people's imaginations, or their political agendas, or their religious prejudices.

Our Lady of Fatima warned us that if we did not heed her message and offer prayer and penance for peace in the world, there would come another and more terrible world war. She also foretold that an "evil was beginning in Russia that would spread its errors throughout the world." One of the tactics that the Communists used so effectively was what is called "revisionist history." It is the re-writing of history to accommodate the past to justify their present political or anti-religious philosophy. We have seen examples of this same tactic in the secular press which often now gives us not a balanced view of all the facts but simply an editorialized version of what they want us to believe. The use of the internet as well as the information provided by many popular talk shows have been able to counter somewhat this trend of distorting facts and help people to reach the objective truth.

Dan Brown's book, *The Da Vinci Code* is, in my opinion, a classic example of "revisionist history." It is not the first example and I am sure it will not be the last. Almost thirty years ago a book appeared that tried to claim that Jesus never rose from the dead but that His disciples, wanting to keep the memory of His good life and holy teachings alive, came up with the idea of saying He rose from the dead. For a group of fishermen and other unsophisticated characters to come up with such an amazing fantasy would be incredulous. Yet many people were excited over the book but it eventually faded away!

I predict the same thing will happen to *The Da Vinci Code*. But while it is popular it is important to counter its many distortions with the facts and especially the truths of Christian Revelation. The book, *Rejecting The Da Vinci Code: How a Blasphemous Novel Brutally Attacks Our Lord and the Catholic Church* by the TFP Committee on American Issues is just the book we need to set the record straight.

    The Da Vinci Code novel is filled with distortions, especially sexual distortions and perversions, which have simply been read back into the life of Christ and the history of the Church. We saw this a few years ago with another book that tried to present Jesus as a homosexual. These gross distortions are in great measure the result of the moral confusion and perversion, coupled with an almost obsessive hatred of religion that characterize our times. Part of the blame must also be traced to the fact that many Catholics today are very poorly catechized in their faith. Their lack of clear knowledge of the fundamental truths of the Church makes many of them gullible to believe *The Da Vinci Code*'s distortions, because they are unable to distinguish truth from deliberate falsehood. Often today people will claim something as true just because the media says it is. This is especially difficult when an author quotes "experts" to support his distorted claims. In the end, these "experts" are no more than other "revisionists" proclaiming their own distorted agendas.

    I encourage the readers of *Rejecting the Da Vinci Code* to study it well. This fine book provides an issue by issue analysis of the distortions of Catholic teaching found in *The Da Vinci Code*. It then offers a refutation of these distortions with a clear presentation of true Catholic teaching. This will prove useful in many ways. First, it will strengthen the faith of any Catholic who reads it. Then, it will serve as an apologetic handbook to counter the distortions made by Dan Brown. Finally, it will prove very useful to help anyone who has become confused or begins to question their Catholic faith as a result of *The Da Vinci Code*. I highly recommend this book and commend its authors.

INTRODUCTION
Why We Must Rally Against
The Da Vinci Code

Dan Brown's 2003 novel, *The Da Vinci Code*, has become a runaway bestseller like *Harry Potter*. Now, as with the boy-wizard's dark fantasy, it is being turned into a major Hollywood production.

Much can be said about why books mixing action, mystery and the occult become bestsellers. An attraction to the esoteric and magical is common in times of religious crisis, cultural decadence, and moral and social decay. But we will not discuss that here.

We will focus instead on *The Da Vinci Code*. Some might see it as just another frivolous novel to while away time at the doctor's office or on the train. We see it in a far different light.

TWO DECADES OF ASSAULT
ON THE CATHOLIC FAITH

Throughout the world, a wave of blasphemous novels, "art" exhibits, films and theater plays has pounded the defenses of the Christian soul for twenty-odd years, weakening and shaking the Faith within.

Some notorious examples of these blasphemies arc:
- Jean-Luc Goddard's *Hail Mary* (1985)
- Martin Scorsese's *The Last Temptation of Christ* (1988)
- Terrence McNally's *Corpus Christi* (1998)
- Paul Rudnick's *The Most Fabulous Story Ever Told* (1998)
- Kevin Smith's *Dogma* (1999)
- Alma Lopez's *Our Lady* (2000)
- Faith Soloway's *Jesus Has Two Mommies* (2001)
- Carlos Carrera's *The Crime of Father Amaro* (2002) and now,
- Dan Brown's *The Da Vinci Code*.

Attacking the sacred person of Our Lord Jesus Christ—the very foundation of Christianity—this unrelenting wave of blasphemy aims to destroy Christianity itself. And since, apart from psychopathic cases, no one derives pleasure from simply destroying something, this goal must include a replacement of Christianity. But until now it was unclear what was to replace it if this worldwide anti-Christian effort succeeded.

THE DA VINCI CODE: REPLACING
CHRISTIANITY WITH NEO-PAGAN GNOSTICISM

The Da Vinci Code makes clear the ultimate goal of this blasphemous campaign: Christianity is to be replaced with age-old paganism and its religion par excellence, Gnosticism.

Like Martin Scorsese with *The Last Temptation of Christ*, Dan Brown takes up again the blasphemous story of a romantic relationship between Our Lord and Saint Mary Magdalene. Brown however goes much further. He repeats old anticlerical criticisms of the Church and presents Gnostic fantasies as the true religion and the authentic Christianity established by Our Lord. Accusing Saint Peter and all the Popes and bishops of the Church for 2,000 years of "the greatest cover-up in History,"[1] he extols untenable Gnostic myths about God, Creation and Redemption that the Apostles and Fathers of the Church denounced and refuted in the early centuries of the Church.

THE DA VINCI CODE:
ALTERING THE COURSE OF HISTORY?

One of the movie's trailers aptly illustrates the psychological climate the novel creates. With New Age music in the background, a mystery-laden voice speaks of a "message that has been hidden for centuries," "a secret that could change the

---

1. Dan Brown, *The Da Vinci Code* (New York: Doubleday, 2003), p. 249. Hereafter referenced as *DVC*.

Gnosticism: A Summary

Gnosis, or Gnosticism, is a religion that attributes the creation of the universe and man to an evil god, the Demiurge, whom Gnostics identify with the God of the Bible. The Demiurge imprisoned a divine particle in man. Gnostics claim that man's salvation consists in liberating the divine particle by illumination, a special kind of knowledge (Gnosis). Gnostics despise the body and all matter since these entrap divine particles, stopping them from reintegrating in the non-personal fullness of divinity.[2]

2. See Chapter 11 – Gnosticism: The Devil's False Wisdom.

course of mankind forever," and concludes with "No matter what you have read, no matter what you believe, the journey has just begun."[3]

The secret mentioned in the trailer, the basis for Dan Brown's novel, is the radically subversive claim that "almost everything our fathers taught us about Christ is false."[4] *The Da Vinci Code*, as the new and true Gospel, will show us Christ as He really was and the authentic tenets of Christianity in their true context.[5]

3. Available at movies.apple.com/movies/sony_pictures/da_vinci_code/ da_vinci_ code_m480.mov.
4. *DVC*, p. 235.
5. Numerous Catholic, Protestant, Jewish and even non-religious writers have denounced *The Da Vinci Code*'s occultist and anti-Christian nature and its historical, theological and artistic errors. See, for example, Carl E. Olson and Sandra Miesel, *The Da Vinci Hoax: Exposing the Errors in* The Da Vinci Code (San Francisco: Ignatius Press, 2004); *Catholic Answers*, "Cracking *The Da Vinci Code*," www.catholic.com/library/cracking_da_vinci_code.asp; Bruce Boucher, "Does *The Da Vinci Code* Crack Leonardo?" *The New York Times*, Aug. 3, 2003; Aviad Kleinberg, "The Feminist Mystique," *Haaretz Daily*, Nov. 7, 2003.

REPARATION AND DEDICATED OPPOSITION

That is why we must rally against *The Da Vinci Code*.

No honorable man would stand idly by while his mother is derided as a prostitute.

Likewise, no true Catholic can shrug off apathetically the massive publicity and promotion surrounding *The Da Vinci Code* with its blasphemous denial of the Divinity of Our Lord Jesus Christ and its base accusations that the Popes and Holy Mother Church adulterated the truth about Our Lord and the deposit of our Faith for 2,000 years.

Just as the honorable man does his utmost to uphold his mother's good name, so must we uphold the Church's honor. Everyone can offer genuine reparation. Books, articles and letters to the editor are excellent ways to voice what should be a universal indignation. This indignation must overflow into the streets as well, in peaceful protests outside theaters showing the movie. We must proclaim loud and clear that, contrary to the false accusations leveled against Her, the Catholic Church has been, is, and will ever be faithful to Her Divine Founder and Spouse.

Through this prudent but fearless struggle we will be fulfilling the vows we made to Our Lord on the day of our Baptism. At the end of it, may we be able to say with the Psalmist, "I have loved, O Lord, the beauty of Thy house; and the place where Thy glory dwelleth."[6]

---

6.   Psalm 25:8. All biblical quotations are from *ScripTours Online Douay-Rheims Bible*, www.scriptours.com/bible/.

PART I
The Da Vinci Code
Deception and Forgery

CHAPTER 1
An Occult "History" in the Form of a Thriller

People who would never leaf through a book of religious instruction are often only too willing to read a thriller in which, amid the suspense, adventure and mystery, a novelist puts forth the tenets and history of a religion. Caught up in the excitement of the plot, such readers easily assimilate at least part of the book's religious message.

A HIDDEN GNOSTIC MESSAGE

The Da Vinci Code is such a book, and it has become a worldwide bestseller. Its message is Gnostic and anti-Catholic.

Throughout its pages of breathless suspense and action, Brown claims the New Testament is a tool of the Church to mislead people about Christ. For his account of Christ's life, he relies on heretical sources such as the Nag Hammadi collection of Gnostic texts found in Egypt in 1945. He quotes from "The Gospel of Philip" and "The Gospel of Mary Magdalene," alleging they are "the **earliest** Christian records" and the "**unaltered** gospels."[1]

We will analyze his misleading statements later. For now, we simply cite them to show that *The Da Vinci Code* has a religious message.

THE DA VINCI CODE GAINED ACCEPTANCE AS A NOVEL

Dan Brown presents *The Da Vinci Code* as a novel. He even chose "A Novel" for the book's subtitle. As a result, the book had a wider readership among the public and less scholarly criticism from historians and theologians than it would have otherwise.

---

1. *DVC*, pp. 245–248. (Our emphasis.)

However, Brown disregards a basic distinction between the novel and other fiction genres like fantasy and satire, namely plausibility of characters and situations and respect for the historical reality.

As we will see in the next chapter, he disfigures his Catholic characters, turning them into gross caricatures disconnected from the real Catholic world.

BROWN CLAIMS TO BE FACTUAL AND HISTORICAL

Dan Brown titled page one "Fact." In this unusual introduction, Brown informs the reader that a Priory of Sion not only exists but dates from 1099. He offers as proof *Les Dossiers Secrets*, parchments discovered in 1975 at the French equivalent of the Library of Congress, the Bibliothèque Nationale.[2] He ends this "Fact" page with a sweeping statement on the accuracy of his descriptions.[3]

With this claim he grows in credibility in the reader's mind, which is being prepared to accept the Gnostic message behind the unfolding story.

• A GNOSTIC MIXTURE OF HISTORY AND FICTION

The claim creates the impression that Brown wrote a historical novel, when in fact he has swept aside serious history and accepted in its place what could be called Gnostic fiction-history.

The merit of undisputed documents is denied outright since History reflects only the views of those who prevail.[4] Scorning history, Brown does not base his work on documentation that can be analyzed according to the principles of internal and external criticism to establish the authenticity, integrity and veracity of events. He bases *The Da Vinci Code* instead on the

---

2. See Chapter 10 where Brown's historical claim for the Priory of Sion and *Les Dossiers Secrets* is debunked.
3. Cf. *DVC*, p. 1.
4. Ibid., p. 256.

What is Historical Fiction?

"What is historical fiction? British historical fiction writer Jill Paton Walsh says, 'a novel is a historical novel when it [is] wholly or partly about the public events and social conditions which are the material of history, regardless of the time at which it is written.' These public events and social conditions must be accurately portrayed when used in historical fiction. The author of historical fiction must blend historical facts with imagination and creative style to master his art. He must be a master of the past so as to portray accurately ideas, attitudes, tendencies and themes and weave his story—accurate in all its details—into the thematic materials."[5]

5. Sarah K. Herz, "Using Historical Fiction in the History Classroom," www.cis.yale.edu/ynhti/curriculum/units/1981/cthistory/81.ch.10.x.html. (Our emphasis.)

"intuitions" or "illuminations" of Gnostics and the fantasies of occultists.

• DAN BROWN'S HISTORIANS

The supposed marriage of Our Lord to Saint Mary Magdalene lies at the center of Brown's absurd and blasphemous depiction of Our Lord Jesus Christ. Their offspring would have been the beginning of a divine lineage. To impress credulous readers, Brown has his character Teabing claim that the lineage of Jesus Christ and Mary Magdalene is attested by numerous historians.[6] In support of his claim he lists these sources:

6. *DVC*, p. 253.

- Lynn Picknett and Clive Prince, *The Templar Revelation: Secret Guardians of the True Identity of Christ*;
- Margaret Starbird, *The Woman With The Alabaster Jar: Mary Magdalene and the Holy Grail*;
- Margaret Starbird, *The Goddess in the Gospels: Reclaiming the Sacred Feminine*;
- Michael Baigent, Richard Leigh and Henry Lincoln, *Holy Blood, Holy Grail*.[7]

• MORE CONCERNED WITH FICTION THAN FACT

These books are typical of what we called Gnostic fiction-history. In them, mysticism and imagination replace scholarly research with its strict use of sources and fair interpretation of evidence. For their authors, conventional history makes impossible the grasping of the more subtle realities.

For instance, the authors of *Holy Blood, Holy Grail* advocate using "the spectrum of disciplines known collectively as 'esoterica'—astrology, alchemy, the Cabala, the Tarot, numerology and sacred geometry."[8] They have to acknowledge, however, that historians were critical of the outcome while novelists praised it: "For, unlike the professional historian, the novelist is accustomed to an approach such as ours. He is

---

7. This book's authors are suing Dan Brown for plagiarism (cf. Elizabeth Day, "*Da Vinci Code* Bestseller Is Plagiarism, Authors Claim," *Telegraph*, Mar. 10, 2004, news.telegraph.co.uk/news/main.jhtml?xml=/news/2004/10/03/wvinci03.xml&sSheet=/news/2004/10/03/ixnewstop.html).
8. Michael Baigent, Richard Leigh and Henry Lincoln, *Holy Blood, Holy Grail* (New York: Dell Publishing, 1983), p. 19. Not surprisingly, Dan Brown includes Deike Begg, author of *The Search for the Holy Grail and the Precious Blood*, in the *DVC* bibliography on his web site (www.danbrown.com/novels/davinci_code/resources.html). Begg is listed as a consultant astrologer at the London Faculty of Astrological Studies (www.astrology.org.uk/pages/about_fas/locate_an_astrologer.htm#devon). He is also a "rebirthing" technician. "Essentially, Rebirthing is a breathing therapy in which you consciously **connect to the divine power of the universe** so that it will cleanse and transform you" (www.respiroconsapevole.it/articoli/deike1.html [our emphasis]).

accustomed to synthesizing diverse material, to making connections more elusive than those explicitly preserved in documents."[9]

"Connections more elusive" fall outside the domain of history. But the adepts of Gnostic fiction-history little care; what matters to them is the "interior illumination" of Gnosis. Accordingly, with ease, they replace facts with fiction and "turn" fantasy into reality. To them, fiction is as real as fact. Margaret Starbird, one of Brown's "historians," states:

> My own story of Mary Magdalene and little Sarah, published as a prologue in *The Woman with the Alabaster Jar*, is fiction. I deliberately wrote fiction because I have no hard evidence about the existence of "Sarah"—only a strong intuition that a child of Jesus survived. I told a story of Mary Magdalene fleeing to Egypt after the Crucifixion because the strong "Gnostic" tradition of Magdalene as "the Beloved" comes from there, found hidden in the codices of the Nag Hammadi library. Even if she didn't herself go to Egypt, her "myth" was there.[10]

MYTHS MATTER

In fiction-history, the fact that people believed a given claim can make the claim as good as true. Margaret Starbird again explains:

> Of course, I cannot prove that the tenets of the Grail heresy are true—that Jesus was married or that Mary Magdalen was the mother of his child. I cannot

---

9. Baigent, Leigh and Lincoln, p. 20.
10. Margaret Starbird, *Mary Magdalene: The Beloved*, www.magdalene.org/beloved_essay.php.

even prove that Mary Magdalen was the woman with
the alabaster jar who anointed Jesus at Bethany. But I
can verify that these are tenets of a heresy widely
believed in the Middle Ages; that fossils of the heresy
can be found in numerous works of art and literature;
that it was vehemently attacked by the hierarchy of
the established Church of Rome; and that it survived
in spite of relentless persecution.[11]

THE MESSAGE BEHIND THE PLOT

The Da Vinci Code is not a historical novel. It is a work of
fantasy, a thriller to spread Gnostic beliefs. Its suspense grips
readers who often fail to critique the book's heretical version
of Christ's life.

A superficial Christian mesmerized by its drama hardly
discerns the book's Gnostic propaganda, whose traces can be
as vague as the pattern on the back of a tapestry. However, a
subtle doubt is planted: Could Brown be right? Might the
Church have hidden the true story of Christ for 2,000 years?

We intend to turn the tapestry around to reveal the Gnostic
design, which must be clearly seen, analyzed and rejected in
the light of history and Church teaching.

We will begin by summarizing the plot so the reader can
more easily follow the analysis of the book's attack on Our
Lord Jesus Christ and the Holy Catholic Church.

---

11. Margaret Starbird, *The Woman With The Alabaster Jar: Mary Magdalen and the
Holy Grail* (Rochester, Vt.: Bear & Co., 1993), p. xxi.

Fiction Has Long Served as a Weapon Against Christianity

That *The Da Vinci Code* is presented as fiction does not diminish the gravity of its blasphemous affirmations and untruths against the Catholic Church.

Gnosticism and the Cathar heresy spread in the Middle Ages thanks largely to the songs of troubadours and the knightly romances of the Holy Grail.

The torrent of blood that was shed in France during the French Revolution (1789–1799) was due in part to the fiction of anti-Catholic authors like Voltaire, who undermined the veneration and respect owed to altar and throne.[12]

Alexandre Dumas, Victor Hugo and other novelists and playwrights at times portrayed the Church as an enemy of freedom and thus helped fuel the anti-clerical persecutions of the nineteenth century.[13]

Here in America, anti-Catholic fiction—particularly the "runaway nun" literature genre—fanned the flames of nativist persecution against the Church.[14] Among the many inflammatory stories is Maria Monk's *The Awful*

---

12. Voltaire's motto was "Ecrasez l'infame!" (Crush the Infamous Thing!) "L'infame" was the Church. (Cf. "Great Minds: Fançois-Marie Arouet de Voltaire," www.secularhumanism.org/library/fi/mcelroy_20_1.htm.)
13. Victor Hugo had no qualms portraying the devil as good in his fiction. "Like other Romantic writers, Hugo was interested in Spiritism, and he experimented with table-tapping. After a number of fruitless efforts, his table gave him the final title of *Les Misérables*. Among Hugo's most ambitious works was an epic poem, *La Fin de Satan*, a study of Satan's fall and the history of the universe. Satan is presented [as a] more complex character than merely the embodiment of the evil, but when Milton saw in *Paradise Lost* in Satan's revolt tragic, cosmic grandeur, Hugo brings forth the horror elements. The poem was never completed" ("Victor Hugo," Classical Reader web site, www.classicreader.com/author.php/aut.68/).
14. Cf. Joseph G. Mannard, "American Anti-Catholicism and its Literature," www.geocities.com/chiniquy/Literature.html.

Disclosures of the Hotel Dieu Nunnery. Although presented as true and factual, Monk's tale was just sordid fantasy.[15]

Far from inconsequential, fiction is a most powerful weapon in the Cultural War. Writing to a German sociologist in 2003, the future Pope Benedict XVI underscored the harm that fiction can bring.

> It is good that you enlighten us on the Harry Potter matter, for these are subtle seductions that are barely noticeable, and precisely because of that have a deep effect and corrupt the Christian faith in souls even before it could properly grow.[16]

God did not give us imagination to blaspheme Him or to distort the Faith. Like all our powers of body and soul, this creative power of our mind should be placed at the service of truth, beauty and virtue. Our imagination should be a means to help us understand better the work of Creation and the dogmas of our Faith.

---

15. Cf. Ruth Hughes, "The Awful Disclosures of Maria Monk," www.english.upenn.edu/~traister/hughes.html.
16. Letter from Cardinal Ratzinger to Gabriele Kuby, www.gabrielekuby.de/resonanz.html.

CHAPTER 2
Catholic Villains and Occultist Heroes

We will now provide a brief overview of the novel's plot and characters as they relate to our analysis.

A LIBERAL POPE, OPUS DEI AND A KILLER "MONK"

A conservative Pope friendly to the Catholic organization Opus Dei dies. His replacement is liberal and opposed to the religious group. The new Pope, through grossly caricatured cardinals,[1] tells the Opus Dei bishop that the organization has lost its standing within the Church.[2]

Bishop Aringarosa, the fictitious Opus Dei prelate, is an amoral fool. He allows himself to be duped by a stranger he thinks will help him regain power in the Church. Over the phone, he makes a deal with the stranger, with whom he never meets.

The stranger promises the prelate the "Holy Grail" in exchange for the services of a member of Opus Dei who will obey him blindly. The prelate orders an Opus Dei member, an escaped criminal he himself converted to the Faith, to follow the stranger's every command.

Nearly impossible to miss, this albino killer dresses up as a Kafkaesque monk when committing his crimes.[3]

THE PRIORY OF SION

The Priory of Sion is said to be a secret society founded by Godfrey of Bouillon at the time of the First Crusade (1096–1099). It worships Mary Magdalene as a goddess. The Order of Knights Templar was the Priory's army.

The Priory is responsible for protecting a secret the Church

---

1. Cf. *DVC*, pp. 173.
2. Ibid., p. 415.
3. Ibid., p. 31.

Opus Dei

Opus Dei is a personal prelature of the Catholic Church that brings together priests and laity to strive for perfection "in and through their everyday activities" according to their state in life. Fr. Josemaria Escrivá de Balaguer founded the organization in Spain in 1928. John Paul II canonized him in 2002.

Brown calls his Opus Dei killer a "monk" 36 times and insinuates that celibate Opus Dei members are monks and dress as such. Opus Dei members are not monks and do not dress as monks.

had done everything to hide. The secret is that Jesus married and had a child with Mary Magdalene; He wanted her, not Saint Peter, to lead the Church; and the Catholic Church's teachings are not those of Christ.

Unlike the Holy Grail of medieval legend, the Holy Grail in the story is not the chalice in which Our Lord consecrated wine on Holy Thursday[4] but the blood of Jesus, meaning blood royal or lineage. Mary Magdalene was supposedly the true "chalice" of Christ's blood, because she carried Christ's child in her womb.[5]

Down through the centuries, the Priory of Sion is the protector of the divine offspring against the fury of the Church. However, the Church succeeded in killing the Merovingian King Dagobert in its attempt to extinguish the Jesus-Mary Magdalene lineage, to which, so the story goes, he belonged.

DESTRUCTION OF THE KNIGHTS TEMPLAR

Brown repeats the customary allegations made against the

---

4. Cf. Arthur F.J. Remy, s.v. "The Holy Grail," *The Catholic Encyclopedia* (New York: McGraw-Hill Book Company, 1967), Vol. 6, pp. 919–921.
5. Cf. *DVC*, pp. 254–258.

Templars: They professed esoteric doctrines, practiced occult ceremonies, adored a pagan god of fertility, and so on.[6]

In the novel, the Knights Templar discovered documents in the ruins of Solomon's Temple confirming that Godfrey of Bouillon descended from Jesus and Mary Magdalene. The Knights blackmailed the Vatican with this information and became extremely powerful. This is why Pope Clement V would have abolished the Order in 1312.[7]

LEONARDO DA VINCI AND MARY MAGDALENE

According to Brown, Leonardo da Vinci, Isaac Newton, "Father of Modern Physics," romanticist Victor Hugo, and film-maker and poet Jean Cocteau were Grand Masters of the Priory of Sion. Da Vinci left clues to the Priory's secret in his art, especially in his famous painting of the Last Supper, where a beardless Saint John next to Our Lord is actually Mary Magdalene—one more "sign" of the marriage between Jesus and Mary Magdalene.

AN OCCULTIST SCENARIO

Brown weaves these unlikely characters and subplots into his main tale, where Jacques Saunière, curator of the Louvre in Paris, is shot in the museum by the albino "monk." Besides Grand Master of the Priory, Saunière is a descendant of Jesus and Mary Magdalene through "Sarah" and, of course, the Merovingian kings.

Fatally wounded, Saunière uses his last moments to leave a message for his granddaughter, Sophie Neveu. Staging an occultist scene, he undresses, lies on his back and paints in his own blood a pentacle on his abdomen. With invisible ink he draws a circle around his body and writes on the floor a series

---

6. Ibid., 316.
7. Ibid., pp. 158–160.

of numbers, two enigmatic expressions, "O, Draconian devil!
Oh, lame saint!" and an instruction that Sophie find Robert
Langdon, a Harvard professor of Religious Symbolism who
happens to be in Paris.

The American immediately becomes a suspect. Bezu Fache,
a Catholic police chief investigating the case and possibly
linked to Opus Dei, does his best to incriminate him. Sophie,
drawing on her expertise as a police cryptographer, saves
Langdon from Fache's clutches.

Their flight from the French police becomes a quest for the
Holy Grail that continues until the novel's conclusion.

CHAPTER 3
The Gospel According to Brown:
A Mortal Christ and a Divine Magdalene

Dan Brown's book is really about the Gnostic rendition of the life of Christ, Who is mentioned by the name of Jesus 96 times.[1]

TWO THOUSAND YEARS
OF COVER-UP, CRIME AND LIES

The basic premise of Brown's story is that "almost everything our fathers taught us about Christ is false."[2] We are victims of "the greatest cover-up in human history."[3]

According to Brown, Constantine deified Jesus for political reasons. During the Council of Nicea, the emperor forced the bishops to declare the Divinity of Christ. Brown affirms that until then Christians had never considered Jesus as God. Sure, He had founded the Church, but He was a man like everyone else.[4]

To impose the "myth" of Christ's Divinity, Constantine ordered the making of a new bible:

> The Bible is a product of man…not of God.
> The modern Bible was compiled and edited by men who possessed a political agenda—to promote the divinity of the man Jesus Christ.[5]

THE REAL DIVINE FIGURE—MARY MAGDALENE

Denying the Divinity of Christ and the Divine inspiration of Scripture, Brown presents "the *other* side of the Christ story"[6]—the Gnostic myth, with its mantra of the sacred feminine and the primeval goddess Sophia. As we will see, Sophia

---

1. The Church is mentioned 205 times and the Vatican 60 times.
2. *DVC*, p. 235.
3. Ibid., p. 249.
4. Ibid.
5. Ibid., pp. 231, 234.
6. Ibid., p. 256. (Emphasis in the original.)

is identified with Mary Magdalene. According to Brown, the marriage of this "goddess" and the man Jesus of Nazareth is "part of the historical record,"[7] and they had a daughter named Sarah.[8]

Francis Cardinal George has pointed out the inanity of such speculation: "Jesus isn't God but Mary Magdalene is a goddess?... If he's not God, why is he married to a goddess?"[9]

SAINT MARY MAGDALENE
AS THE GODDESS SOPHIA

However, that is the context in which Brown asserts that Christ wanted Mary Magdalene—and not Saint Peter—to lead the Church.[10]

Margaret Starbird, one of Brown's "historians,"[11] writes

Among the Gnostic Christians of the first three centuries of the Christian era, it was Mary Magdalene who was honored as the incarnation of the "Sophia."[12]

For the earliest Christians, the goddess in the Gospels was Mary Magdalene.[13]

But to those who now examine them, there can be not the least doubt that the Mary called the Magdalene was the Goddess hidden from the very

---

7. Ibid., p. 245.
8. Ibid. p. 255. As pointed out in Chapter 1, the story of Sarah, the "daughter" of Jesus and Mary Magdalene, is pure fiction.
9. Cathleen Falsani, "Cardinal Takes a Crack at *The Da Vinci Code*," *Chicago Sun-Times*, Jan. 9, 2004, www.suntimes.com/special_sections/falsani/cst-nws-fals09.html.
10. Cf. *DVC*, p. 248.
11. "In October 2003, Dan Brown acknowledged to me that Ms. Starbird's book *The Woman with the Alabaster Jar* was a significant influence on his novel" (Ed Conroy, "Resurrecting Mary Magdalene," *National Catholic Reporter*, Jul. 15, 2005).
12. Starbird, *The Feminine Face of Christianity* (Wheaton, Ill.: Quest Books Theosophical Publishing House, 2003), p. 116.
13. Starbird, *The Goddess in the Gospels* (Rochester, Vt.: Bear & Co., 1998), p. 9.

beginning in the Christian Gospels![14]

The Da Vinci Code's "Mary Magdalene" is simply a version of this Gnostic goddess Sophia. Its Priory is the remnant faithful to the "true" Church despite Catholic persecution.[15]

14. Ibid., p. 141.
15. Cf. *DVC,* p. 255.

CHAPTER 4
The Androgynous Goddess
of Gnostic Eroticism

Know you not that your bodies are the members of Christ?
Shall I then take the members of Christ
and make them the members of an harlot? God forbid.
— 1 Cor. 6:15

Dan Brown makes common cause with radical neopagan feminism in its bid to restore the worship of the sacred feminine.

He claims that Constantine and his successors established patriarchal Christianity, stamping out the ancient goddess worship and denouncing the sacred feminine as evil.[1]

The Church supposedly continued this work, burning no less than five million witches at the stake between the fifteenth and eighteenth centuries.[2]

Brown concludes that the Church's victory over pagan Gnosticism and the sacred feminine is to blame—still today—for unjust wars, the oppression of women, and environmental degradation.[3]

FEMINISM AND GNOSTIC ANDROGYNISM

Radical feminists who turn to Gnosticism to defend their anti-patriarchal views eventually come to the realization that the balance Gnostics advocate between male and female is androgyny. The Gnostic goddess Sophia herself is androgynous.

For example, the collection of Gnostic texts found at Nag Hammadi, Egypt, in 1945 and cited by Brown contains numerous references to the androgynous goddess. One reads in "The

---

1. Cf. *DVC*, p. 124.
2. Ibid., pp. 124-125.
3. Ibid., p. 126.

A Gnostic "Christian" Feminism

In the confusion after the Second Vatican Council, in which all sorts of "experiments" were allowed, militant feminist thought penetrated deeply in Catholic circles. "Catholic" feminists followed the general trend of the movement, which eventually took them down the path of Gnosticism.[4]

According to Donna Steichen, feminist theologian Rosemary Ruether deems Gnostic writings "more reliable than the 'patriarchal' canon of Sacred Scripture."[5]

Fr. William P. Saunders, pastor of Our Lady of Hope Parish in Potomac Falls, Virginia, comments:

> This movement uses the teachings found in Gnostic writings to support their desire for female priesthood, contraception, abortion, and deviant lifestyles. They focus their worship on Sophia, the feminine god, not the Heavenly Father or Jesus, true God who became true man.[6]

4. Cf. Donna Steichen, *Ungodly Rage – The Hidden Face of Catholic Feminism* (San Francisco: Ignatius Press, 1991).
5. Ibid., p. 302.
6. Fr. William P. Saunders, "Gnostic Gospels," *Catholic Herald*, Oct. 23, 2003, www.catholicherald.com/saunders/03ws/ws031023.htm.

Exegesis on the Soul": "As long as she was alone with the father, she was virgin and in form androgynous;"[7] and in "The Aprocryphon of John," "She became the womb of everything for it is she who is prior to them all, the Mother-Father, the first man, the holy Spirit, the thrice-male, the thrice-powerful, the

7. James M. Robinson, ed., *The Nag Hammadi Library* (San Francisco: Harper Collins Publishers, 1990), p. 192.

thrice-named androgynous one."[8] "The Apocalypse of Adam" states:

> From the nine Muses one [Sophia] separated away. She came to a high mountain and spent (some) time seated there, so that she desired herself alone in order to become androgynous. She fulfilled her desire and became pregnant from her desire.[9]

In "The Trimophic Protennoia" (The Three-formed First Thought) the goddess affirms: "I am androgynous. [I am Mother (and) I am] Father since [I copulate] with myself."[10] In "The Gospel According to Thomas" women must become men to be saved.

> Simon Peter said to them, "Let Mary leave us, for women are not worthy of life." Jesus said, "I myself shall lead her in order to make her male, so that she too may become a living spirit resembling you males. For every woman who will make herself male will enter the kingdom of heaven."[11]

According to "The Gospel of Philip" (cited by Brown to prove that Jesus and Mary Magdalene were married), the first human was androgynous and the loss of androgyny was the cause of evil in the world:

---

8. Ibid., p. 107.
9. Ibid., p. 284. The editor of *The Nag Hammadi Library* in English explains that "square brackets indicate a lacuna in the manuscript. When the text cannot be reconstructed, three dots are placed within the brackets, regardless of the size of the lacuna.... Parentheses indicate material supplied by the editor or translator. Although this material may not directly reflect the text being translated, it provides useful information for the reader" (p. xv).
10. Ibid., p. 519.
11. Ibid., p. 138.

When Eve was still in Adam death did not exist.
When she was separated from him death came into
being. If he [sic] enters again and attains his former
self, death will be no more.[12]

THE FUSION OF MALE AND FEMALE

Although the term "androgynous" occurs only four times in
The Da Vinci Code and "androgyny" only once, androgynous
unity is mentioned throughout the book.[13]

For instance, the novel hero Robert Langdon explains the
masculine and feminine dimension of all things to the heroine
Sophie (who bears the goddess's name). The equal-armed
cross,[14] the star of David,[15] the rose,[16] the paintings of
Leonardo da Vinci,[17] the name Jehovah,[18] all are given androgynous connotations. As he unveils the "mysteries" of Leonardo
da Vinci's *Mona Lisa*, Langdon says the painting discreetly
conveys a fusion of male and female.[19]

This portraying of androgyny in the *Mona Lisa* is "con-
firmed" by "Mona Lisa" being an anagram of the names of
Amon and Isis, Egyptian gods of masculine and feminine sexuality.[20] As for the woman in the painting, Brown suggests it is
Leonardo da Vinci himself.[21]

Brown will repeatedly refer to the androgynous principle,
especially in its reflection in da Vinci's paintings.[22]

---

12. Ibid., p. 150. The gender confusion is in the original. For androgynists, "he" and
    "she" are interchangeable.
13. Cf. *DVC*, p. 36.
14. Ibid., pp. 139, 145, 168, 171, 172.
15. Ibid., p. 435, 446.
16. Ibid., p. 255.
17. Ibid., pp. 119, 120, 244.
18. Ibid., p. 309.
19. Ibid., p. 120.
20. Ibid., p. 121.
21. Ibid., p. 120.
22. See, for example, *DVC* pages 45, 95, 113, 119–121, 168–169, 231, 244, 316.

Brown's Lack of Intellectual Seriousness

Brown's idea that "Mona Lisa" is an anagram of the names of the Egyptian fertility deities Amon and Isis is but one example of his lack of intellectual seriousness. "Mona" (with double n in Italian and a single n in its anglicized form) became a title of courtesy in late medieval Italy. Mona Lisa means My lady Lisa.[23]

Da Vinci biographer Giorgio Vasari (1511–1574) affirmed that the woman in the painting is Lisa Gherardini, wife of Francesco del Giocondo. Hence the painting is known also as *La Gioconda or La Joconda*.[24]

---

23. See the entry *mònna* in *De Mauro—Il dizionario della lingua italiana*, www.demauroparavia.it/71257.
24. Cf. Giorgio Vasari, Lives of the Artists, "Lionardo da Vinci," www.fordham.edu/halsall/basis/vasari/vasari14.htm.

RETURNING TO INITIAL "WHOLENESS" THROUGH THE SEXUAL ACT

According to some Gnostics, the sexual act is sacred and restores "wholeness," the unity between the sexes that they claim existed in the first human (Adam-Eve). They also contend that this mystic-carnal union is the means to attain Gnostic knowledge and immersion in the divine.

Brown emphasizes this Gnostic teaching on the sexual act in a dialogue between Langdon and his students. Wanting to make sure he understood correctly, one of the students asks Langdon if he meant they should have sexual intercourse instead of going to church. In reply, Langdon repeats the essence of the Gnostic teaching that the student should see sexual intercourse as a mystical act that will enable him to release the divine spark within him and connect with the divinity.[25]

The truth is another, however. It is the natural law, written by God on the human heart,[26] and the divine law revealed in the New and Old Testaments that teach mankind the true purpose of the sexual act—a teaching the Church transmits infallibly and perennially.

---

25. Ibid., pp. 125, 308-310.
26. Rom. 2:15.

Dissident Catholics Make
Use of *The Da Vinci Code*

Dissident movements in the Catholic Church like the Gnostic portrayal of Saint Mary Magdalene. They often use the great saint as a banner of revolt against a hierarchical Church. It is in this spirit that movements such as Call to Action, We Are Church and Future Church, together with the homosexual movement Dignity, promote a "Feast of Mary of Magdala, Apostle and Church Leader" and present the saint as a feminist leader or even a goddess.[27]

Dan Brown may have had these "Catholics" in mind when he wrote his thriller. They in turn are rejoicing at the advantage their cause can reap from the book's worldwide readership and its production as a movie. A post to Call to Action's discussion board illustrates the point.

> As we are all aware the book by Dan Brown *The Da Vinci Code* is now being made into a movie. Up front this may not seem too important. However I believe that one of the biggest problems the church is facing today is the re awakening of the feminine. This movie can pose a huge   problem since I believe it may be the CATALYST which will give women the nudge they require in order to get the courage to go forth with the movement to RIGHT herself.

---

27. www.cta-usa.org/news9-98/women.html; www.cta-usa.org/news0900/ctareg ions.html; www.cta-usa.org/news0901/magdala.html; www.cta-usa.org/news 200309/magdala.html.

As some may be aware. The book brings up the subject of how the church "demonized" the Goddess (sexuality, symbolism, feminine wisdom, spirituality).[28]

---

28. Call to Action Discussion Board, Apr. 24, 2005, subject: *Da Vinci Code*, www.cta-usa.org/board/phpBB2/viewtopic.php?t=171&sid=3cb3121cd4fce2b900d61fb5504 28012.

CHAPTER 5
Luciferianism in *The Da Vinci Code*?

It is noteworthy that in *The Da Vinci Code* Dan Brown repeats thirteen times the invocation

O, Draconian devil!

Oh, lame saint![1]

This "prayer"—with its invocatory character reinforced by the exclamation mark—first appears as an anagram for "Leonardo da Vinci! The Mona Lisa!" in the secret message the agonizing Grand Master Jacques Saunière writes for his granddaughter Sophie.[2]

Brown himself explains, however, that with these exclamations "Saunière had left a literal reference to the devil."[3]

It is this reference to the devil and its link with Luciferian Gnosticism that we will now consider.

THE DRAGON OF THE APOCALYPSE

"O, Draconian devil!" is an allusion to the great angelic battle Saint John describes in the twelfth chapter of the Apocalypse.

Lucifer—the highest angel according to some, one of the highest according to others— revolted against God, saying, "I will not serve!" A third of the angels joined him. The other angels rallied at Saint Michael's battle cry, "Who is like unto God!" and cast Lucifer and his followers out of heaven into the depths of hell.

> And there was a great battle in heaven, Michael and his angels fought with the dragon, and the dragon fought and his angels: And they prevailed not, neither was their place found any more in heaven. And that

---

1. *DVC*, pp. 43, 44, 46, 47, 81, 91, 97, 98.
2. Ibid., p. 98.
3. Ibid., p. 43.

great dragon was cast out, that old serpent, who is
called the devil and Satan, who seduceth the whole
world; and he was cast unto the earth, and his angels
were thrown down with him.[4]

Satanist groups therefore sometimes refer to themselves as
draconian, that is, as following or worshipping the dragon.[5]

THE FALLEN, WOUNDED GOD/GODDESS

"Oh, lame saint" reflects the doctrine of some Gnostics that
Lucifer or Satan is himself a god, though provisionally "lame"
because of his defeat by the God of the Bible. Sophia's expul-
sion from the Gnostic "heaven" expresses this belief.

As Msgr. E. Amman states, for Luciferians "the devil is a
fallen god but one who kept a great part of his initial power."[6]
Monsignor Amman sees the neo-Manicheans as Gnostic
Luciferians. These heretics migrated from Asia to Bulgaria,
where they were called Bogomiles, and from there to
Dalmatia. Later they moved into northern Italy and southern
France, becoming known as Cathars or Albingensians, after
the Provençal city of Albi, one of their main centers. According
to a Cathar's confession,

> The Cathars believe that the God of heaven, whom
> the holy Church honors, is an unjust God who
> expelled through violence their God Lucifer from
> heaven—whom they call their supreme father—and
> created all visible things and the human body. At the

---

4. Apoc. 12:7–9.
5. Cf. Draconis Blackthorne, *Dracomeroth: The Draconian Bible*, www.geoci-
   ties.com/Athens/Parthenon/2669/DBooks.html;
   www.geocities.com/Paris/Bistro/1368/draconianchurch.html.
6. Msgr. E. Amann, "Luci, "Luci,"Luciferiens," *Dictionnaire de Théologie Catholique* (Paris,
   Letouzey et Ané, 1926) Vol. 9, col. 1045.

end of time, Lucifer will recover his empire.[7]

Dan Brown's main "historical" source, *Holy Blood, Holy Grail*, paints the Cathars in a very favorable light, and summarizes their Gnostic dualism thus: "The universe, in short, was the handiwork of a 'usurper god,' the god of evil—or, as the Cathars called him, 'Rex Mundi,' 'King of the World.'"[8]

Brown's other supposedly "historical" but actually occultist authorities—Starbird, Picknett and Prince, etc.—are equally sympathetic to the Cathars.

LUCIFER AND GODDESS WORSHIP

Dan Brown's use of such authors reinforces the idea that Luciferian Gnosticism pervades *The Da Vinci Code*. The title of a new book by Picknett, for instance, is quite suggestive: *The Secret History of Lucifer: Evil Angel or the Secret of Life Itself?*[9]

Amazon.com's description of the book reads:

> Who is Lucifer? For many of us Lucifer and Satan are alternative names for the embodiment of pure evil....
>
> Lynn Picknett explains that the horned Devil is merely a new incarnation of the old woodland deity Pan, while Lucifer was once a personification of the Morning Star, the planet Venus and its goddess. "He" was therefore originally "she," and a divine representation of love, beauty, and human warmth. Indeed, many ancient goddesses were known as Lucifera, or

---

7. Ibid., col. 1054.
8. Baigent, Leigh and Lincoln, p. 53.
9. Lynn Picknett, *The Secret History of Lucifer: Evil Angel or the Secret of Life Itself?* (New York: Carroll & Graf Publisher, 2005).

"Light-bringer."[10]

Picknett's view is common in Gnostic circles. Here is an example from the *Luciferian Gnosis* webring:

> Lucifer literally means "Light Bearer," is equated with Venus as the Morning Star and is the force of enlightenment. Some of the sites see parallels between Lucifer and figures in other traditions, including the Gnostic Sophia and/or Christ.[11]

The Gnostic Witch Bible, in its section "Gnostic Genesis: the Dragon's Tale," identifies Lucifer in the Garden of Paradise with Sophia.

> Now Lucifer-Sophia, or Sophia-Lucifer for She could not yet tell Herself apart, was more wise and coherent than the rest of the manifestations She had become, so conceiving a notion, She inhabited a serpent. She said to the woman knowingly, "You may do what you wish in this Paradise?"[12]

In its introduction *The Gnostic Witch Bible* states that Lucifer is not evil, but an angel of light, an angel of mercy who helps man see his own hidden divinity and escape from the material universe created by the God of the Bible into the ethereal and divine realm of the Alien God, the fullness of light, or Pleroma.

---

10. "Book Description," *Amazon.com*, http://www.amazon.com/exec/obidos/ASIN/ 078671560X/ref=pd_sxp_f/103-1374332-0710241.
11. "Luciferian Gnosis," http://n.webring.com/hub?ring=luciferiangnosis.
12. "Gnostic Genesis: the Dragon's Tale," *The Gnostic Witch Bible*, www.lightbringer.com/Gnosis/Mystical_Tales/dragons_genesis.html, Chap. 3.

This Alien God is foreign to our existence, neither its creator nor its keeper. It is the Source of all that is or ever can be. Lucifer whispers to us this secret so that we can escape from the prison that this universe is.... Lucifer, like the rest of us, seeks to reach the higher realm of the Pleroma but the Light of divinity that shines within each of us restrains Lucifer from leaving. This Angel of Mercy, the loftiest of archangels and regent of the planet Venus, remains to see that each of us escape too.[13]

THE CHURCH IS THE ENEMY

In *The Da Vinci Code*, the Church invented original sin and the figure of Satan to destroy the sacred feminine and goddess worship.

"It was *man*, not God, who created the concept of 'original sin.'"[14]

The modern belief in a *horned* devil known as Satan could be traced back to Baphomet and the Church's attempts to recast the horned fertility god as a symbol of evil.[15]

In short, according to Brown, the Catholic Church "had subjugated women, banished the Goddess, burned nonbelievers, and forbidden the pagan reverence to the sacred feminine."[16]

THE CHURCH UPHELD THE DIGNITY OF WOMEN

The accusation that the Church subjugated women contra-

---

13. "Introduction," *The Gnostic Witch Bible*, www.lightbringer.com/Gnosis/ Gnoses/introduction.html.
14. *DVC*, p. 238. (Emphasis in the original.)
15. Ibid., p. 37. (Emphasis in the original.)
16. Ibid., p. 239.

dicts the historical truth that the Church's influence led to a greater respect for their dignity.

The Church has always taught that both man and woman are created in the image and likeness of God, and each reflects the sacredness of the Creator.

This sacredness is such that Saint Paul says husband and wife should model their love according to Christ's love for the Church: "Husbands, love your wives, as Christ also loved the Church."[17]

---

17. Eph. 5:25.

PART II
Setting the Record Straight—The Facts

CHAPTER 6
The God Who Is So Reviled:
The Adorable Person
of Our Lord Jesus Christ

The adorable person of Our Lord Jesus Christ is the very core, the life-giving principle, the unifying force of the Catholic Church. He is, as He said, "the way, and the truth, and the life."[1]

The world may measure someone's importance by his wealth, beauty, prestige, strength, intellect, talent. From a Catholic perspective the supreme measure is union with Our Lord.

This explains the Catholic love for the Blessed Virgin Mary, for who is closer to Our Lord than His Blessed Mother? This explains the place accorded in Catholic hearts to Saint Joseph, His foster father, the Apostles and Evangelists, the martyrs, confessors and virgins, and in a special way the Pope, His Vicar on earth. This explains the Catholic life-long striving to better know, love, serve and defend Our Lord Jesus Christ.

GOD'S HUMILITY, MAN'S PRIDE

In their pagan pride, Gnostics over the centuries have been shocked at the idea of a God who, unlike Jupiter hurling lightning bolts on men and living as a libertine on Mount Olympus, chose to share our human weakness and offer Himself as victim for our sins through the Incarnation of the Second Person of the Holy Trinity.

Gnostics fail to accept that, to satisfy Divine Justice offended by our sins, Our Lord Jesus Christ, being God,

---

1. John 14:6.

emptied Himself, taking the form of a servant, being
made in the likeness of men, and in habit found as a
man.

He humbled Himself, becoming obedient unto
death, even to the death of the cross.[2]

This is why Saint Paul proclaims the truth of Christianity as
opposed to the pride of the pagans and the incomprehension of
the Jews, who expected a worldly king.

For the word of the cross, to them indeed that
perish, is foolishness: but to them that are saved, that
is, to us, it is the power of God....

But we preach Christ crucified: unto the Jews
indeed a stumbling block, and unto the Gentiles
foolishness.[3]

THE ALMIGHTY SUBMITTED
TO THE CONSENT OF A VIRGIN

Gnostics also do not accept that God, in His infinite love for
us, associated a mere creature with the work of Redemption by
choosing Mary—a faithful and prudent virgin, unlike the
Sophia of mythology—to be the Mother of the Word Incarnate.

Confounding the proud, the Creator of the Universe, the
Lord of All, the Almighty, humbled Himself to the point of
conditioning the Incarnation to Mary's free consent.

And in the sixth month, the angel Gabriel was sent
from God into a city of Galilee, called Nazareth, to a
virgin espoused to a man whose name was Joseph, of
the house of David: and the virgin's name was Mary.

---

2. Phil. 2:7–8.
3. 1 Cor. 1:18, 23.

And the angel being come in, said unto her: Hail, full of grace, the Lord is with thee: blessed art thou among women.

Who having heard, was troubled at his saying and thought with herself what manner of salutation this should be.

And the angel said to her: Fear not, Mary, for thou hast found grace with God. Behold thou shalt conceive in thy womb and shalt bring forth a son: and thou shalt call his name Jesus. He shall be great, and shall be called the Son of the Most High; and the Lord God shall give unto him the throne of David his father: and he shall reign in the house of Jacob for ever. And of his kingdom there shall be no end.

And Mary said to the angel: How shall this be done, because I know not man?

And the angel answering, said to her: The Holy Ghost shall come upon thee and the power of the Most High shall overshadow thee. And therefore also the Holy which shall be born of thee shall be called the Son of God. And behold thy cousin Elizabeth, she also hath conceived a son in her old age: and this is the sixth month with her that is called barren. Because no word shall be impossible with God.

And Mary said: Behold the handmaid of the Lord: be it done to me according to thy word.[4]

A HUMBLE BIRTH AND LIFE

Man cannot even fathom the immensity of God's universe, yet as Saint Louis de Montfort says,

God-made-man found freedom in imprisoning

---

4. Luke 1:26–38.

himself in her [Mary's] womb. He displayed power in allowing himself to be borne by this young maiden.... He glorified his independence and his majesty in depending upon this lovable virgin in his conception, his birth, his presentation in the temple, and in the thirty years of his hidden life. Even at his death she had to be present so that he might be united with her in one sacrifice and be immolated with her consent to the eternal Father.[5]

Until the end of time, people of all nations will marvel at the birth of the God-man in a cold and desolate stable, alone with Mary and Joseph, "because there was no room for them in the inn."[6]

Seemingly powerless, He fled into Egypt to escape Herod's cruelty, although He had drowned the Pharaoh and his army in the Red Sea to save the Chosen People.

In Nazareth, He led a hidden life, His omnipotence and wisdom unknown to others; yet He had left the sages of the Temple speechless at His teaching.

He had himself baptized in the River Jordan by His forerunner, Saint John the Baptist, as if He were a sinner like us. But He is Innocence itself, the Lamb of God Who takes away the sins of the world.

THE PATH OF THE BEATITUDES

The God-man taught a doctrine of purity and humility, forgiveness of one's enemies, and meekness of heart. During the Sermon on the Mount, He instructed us on how to reach His kingdom in serene words that echo across the centuries:

---

5. St. Louis de Montfort, *God Alone – The Collected Writings of St. Louis Marie de Montfort* (Bay Shore, N.Y.: Montfort Publications, 1987) p. 295.
6. Luke 2:7.

Blessed are the poor in spirit: for theirs is the kingdom of heaven.

Blessed are the meek: for they shall possess the land.

Blessed are they that mourn: for they shall be comforted.

Blessed are they that hunger and thirst after justice: for they shall have their fill.

Blessed are the merciful: for they shall obtain mercy.

Blessed are the clean of heart: they shall see God.

Blessed are the peacemakers: for they shall be called the children of God.

Blessed are they that suffer persecution for justice' sake: for theirs is the kingdom of heaven.

Blessed are ye when they shall revile you, and persecute you, and speak all that is evil against you, untruly, for my sake:

Be glad and rejoice for your reward is very great in heaven. For so they persecuted the prophets that were before you.[7]

A CRUCIFIED GOD

On Palm Sunday, multitudes acclaimed the God-man as He entered Jerusalem, laying branches before Him, hailing Him as the Son of David. Nevertheless He knew that in a few days He would stumble through the same streets under a shower of insults, despised as a criminal, carrying His cross to the place of execution.

To save men and restore them to freedom as children of God, He allowed Himself to be betrayed by one of His own apostles, arrested in the middle of the night, tied with ropes and chains, and dragged before the High Priest and the Sanhedrin as an abject malefactor.

---

7. Matt. 5:3–12.

He endured a most brutal scourging ordered by a Roman prefect who had proclaimed His innocence.

He, at whose command the winds and the sea were stilled and the dead returned to life, was crowned with thorns, spat upon, and mocked by soldiers.

They stripped Him of his clothes, while He continued to envelop the whole universe in His Providence.

He accepted to be nailed to a cross and to hang there between two common thieves, one of whom He promised to take that very day to paradise.

God had made water flow in the desert for His people. Now, the God-man thirsted mightily from the great loss of blood.

To test Abraham, God had asked him to sacrifice his only son Isaac, but then had sent an angel to prevent the boy's death. God did not do the same, however, for His Beloved Son, Who was immolated for our sins.

After agonizing for three hours amid the jeers of a mob that challenged Him to descend from the Cross so they might believe, Jesus assured us from the depths of His spiritual abandonment that He had paid the price of our redemption. In a loud voice He surrendered His soul to the Eternal Father, and died.

It is this Adorable Jesus that Dan Brown strikes at in *The Da Vinci Code*. It is this Jesus that every Catholic worthy of the name must rise up to console, following the example of the Blessed Mother, Saint Mary Magdalene and the others with her at the foot of the Cross.

Holy Eucharist or Holy Grail?

What could be more marvelous to a person with the inestimable gift of faith than the Sacrament of the Eucharist? Under the appearances of bread and wine the Body and Blood of Jesus Christ are really and substantially present, offered up in sacrifice and distributed for the nourishment of souls.

It is a mystery and a miracle continuously renewed before our eyes. We must open our souls to understand its meaning and reap its benefits.

MARVELLING FAITH VS. FANTASTIC SUPERSTITION

Unlike the angels, man is endowed with sensibility. Therefore the Savior instituted visible signs that impart the grace they signify: the sacraments. Likewise He founded a visible Church with visible elements such as clergy, liturgy and ceremonial. These visible elements are vivified by an invisible element: grace.

Without this supernatural, invisible element, we neither understand the visible element nor give it its due value. Faith opens our eyes to this marvelous reality of a life of grace that sanctifies and renews all things. Grace thus satisfies the natural human propensity for the sublime, which enables us to transcend the mundane and broaden our horizons beyond the merely natural.

When faith is weak, distorted, or nonexistent, sensibility, instead of reason fortified by grace, dominates. People lose touch with authentic sublimity, which requires asceticism of the will and submission of the intellect. They give themselves up to fantasy and superstition. They pursue a "marvelousness" that speaks directly to their sensibility, satisfies their whims, caters to their pride and gives free rein to their sensuality. All of which prepare them psychologically and morally to accept the irrationality of false mysticism.

FROM THE HOLY EUCHARIST
TO AN OCCULTIST HOLY GRAIL

Through this subtle process many in all epochs abandoned the sublimity of the faith only to adopt a blind and childish belief in false marvelousness.

Consequently, over time the pious desire to find the chalice used by Our Lord when He instituted the Holy Eucharist degenerated into the delirium of fantasy and occultism found in Gnostic-leaning authors. In their writings the chalice stands for a Mary Magdalene that is not the Magdalene of the Gospels, but a Gnostic goddess who married Christ, starting a lineage that we are to believe includes the French Merovingian dynasty (481 to 751) and survives to this day.

CHAPTER 7
The Real Saint Mary Magdalene

*"Many sins are forgiven her,
because she hath loved much."*
—Luke 7:47

The Da Vinci Code portrayal of Saint Mary Magdalene is that of feminist Gnosticism.[1]

In the novel, when Sophie Neveu refers to the saint as a harlot, Sir Leigh Teabing replies that this mischaracterization was spread by the Church to cover up the fact that Mary Magdalene was Jesus's wife and Sarah's mother.

BROWN'S DISTORTION AND DEFAMATION

Actually, the Church has presented Saint Mary Magdalene as a repentant sinner who, treated by the Savior with great mercy, attained a high degree of sanctity by the intensity of her contrition, faith and love.[2]

For this reason, devotion to her was always extremely popular in the Church, especially in an age of faith, when people understood the beauty of repentance and penance.

AN ADMIRABLE EXAMPLE OF CONVERSION

In keeping with Saints Augustine, Cyprian, Gregory the Great and Bernard, the Scripture scholar Fr. Cornelius à Lapide (1567–1637) explains:

> Undoubtedly, Christ allowed St. Mary Magdalene to wallow in lust so that, once she was cleansed, His grace would stand out in her so that, from a sinner, she would become an angelic creature; for the greater the

---

1. Cf. Chapter 4—The Androgynous Goddess of Gnostic Eroticism.
2. "Many sins are forgiven her, because she hath loved much. But to whom less is forgiven, he loveth less" (Luke 7:47).

illness, the more it makes stand out the power of the doctor that heals it. Nor does the fact of having been a sinner destroy the honor of Magdalene, but rather increases it: because however great and constant she was in sinning, she showed an even greater courage to break free from sin and to do penance. Thus, God gave Magdalene as a living example of perfect penance to all sinners so they do not despair facing the enormity of their sins but rather confide in God's immense mercy. For as Saint Paul teaches, "Christ Jesus came into the world to save sinners, of whom I am the first. But for this cause have I obtained mercy: that in me first Christ Jesus might show forth all patience, for the information of them that shall believe in him unto life everlasting" (1 Tim. 1:15).[3]

A LIFE SHROUDED IN MYSTERY

The Gospels give only a general profile of Saint Mary Magdalene, leaving us with an image that is both mysterious and sublime.

This is why Church scholars differed from the beginning on how to interpret some New Testament passages that seem to refer to her, especially Saint Luke's passage on the repentant woman.[4] However, beginning with Saint Gregory the Great at the end of the sixth century, the thesis that Saint Mary Magdalene was the repentant sinner prevailed at least in the West and molded the piety of the faithful, as well as literature and arts.

The Church made no official pronouncement on the matter. She did, however, accept the identification of Saint Mary Magdalene with the repentant sinner both in the Mass and in the

---

3. Cornelius à Lapide, *Commentaria in Scripturam Sacram, Commentaria in Lucam* (Paris: Ludovicum Vivès Bibliopola Editor, 1881), Vol. 16, p. 121.
4. Luke 7:36–50.

Divine Office until the 1969 liturgical reform. The feastday Mass on July 22 was that of "Saint Mary Magdalene, Penitent," and the Gospel reading was Saint Luke's narrative of the sinner who washed Our Lord's feet with her tears, wiped them with her hair, and then anointed them with precious ointment.[5]

Therefore, even if scholars still dispute among themselves, there is no reason to challenge a whole culture of devotion to this saint as a model of conversion and penance that has been fashioned over centuries.[6] This is all the more true since neither scholarly current carries sufficient weight to elicit adhesion in the absence of a definitive Church pronouncement.

Without taking sides in this scholarly debate, we will present the position that has modeled the piety of the faithful, simply to demonstrate that it is not fruit of "mere confusion" as some claim, and even less of a "campaign" against Saint Mary Magdalene as *The Da Vinci Code* would have it.

AN ARDENT SOUL AT THE SERVICE OF GOD

The Gospels place Saint Mary Magdalene among the women who accompanied and served the Divine Master[7] even

---

5. Cf. Luke 7:36 50. *Saint Joseph's Daily Missal* (New York: Catholic Book Publishing Co., 1961), p. 969. The Missal's short biography of the Saint reads: "Mary Magdalene, the sister of Martha and Lazarus, was directly converted from a life of sin by Our Lord Himself. She was one of the few faithful souls who remained with Christ during His agony on the Cross. After our Lord's Resurrection, He appeared to her and told her to announce His Resurrection to the Apostles."

6. Most Scripture scholars today oppose identifying St. Mary Magdalene with the repentant sinner who anointed Christ's feet. Their position is aptly summarized by Fr. Andrés Fernandes, S.J. (*The Life of Christ* [Westminster, Md.: The Newman Press, 1958], pp. 360–363), and by J. E. Fallon ("St. Mary Magdalene," *The New Catholic Encyclopedia*, Vol. 9, pp. 347–349). That the repentant sinner is St. Mary Magdalene is well argued by Fr. Hugh Pope ("St. Mary Magdalene," *The New Catholic Encyclopedia*). This position is sustained by Fr. Cornelius à Lapide, the great exegete, and also by Fr. H. Lesêtre ("Marie Madeleine," *Dictionnaire de la Bible* [Paris: Letozey et Ané, Editeurs, 1912], cols. 809–818).

though seven devils had been expelled from her.[8] She remained faithful and stood by the Cross with Mary Most Holy, Mary Cleophas and Mary Salome.[9] She attended the burial of Christ and was the first witness of the Resurrection, having received the mission of announcing it to the Apostles.[10]

These facts are indisputable since the Evangelists expressly refer to her by name. The doubt arises over whether she was the woman who anointed the feet and head of the Savior.[11]

Saint Luke cites neither the name of the city nor that of the woman, but designates the host that day as Simon the Pharisee. This evangelist is the only one who mentions that the woman was a "sinner in the city."

Saints Matthew, Mark and John name the city as Bethany. However, the first two name the host as Simon the Leper, while Saint John says Our Lord was a guest of Lazarus and his two sisters, Martha and Mary. Saints Matthew and Mark do not name the woman, but Saint John clearly states it was Mary, the sister of Lazarus (Mary of Bethany). Likewise, in the preceding chapter, as he introduces Mary of Bethany he clarifies: "And Mary was she that anointed the Lord with ointment and wiped his feet with her hair: whose brother Lazarus was sick."[12]

Generally, commentators admit that the gesture of anointing the feet and head of the Savior took place on two different occasions: the first, by the repentant sinner in Galilee, and the second in Judea. Since in the phrase above, Saint John refers to an anointing that happened before the one he is about to narrate, that of Judea, many have concluded that he is referring to the Galilee anointing by the repentant sinner, narrated by Saint

7. Luke 8:2–3.
8. Luke 8:2; Mark 16:9.
9. Mark 15:40; Matt. 27:56; John 19:25; Luke 23:49.
10. Matt. 27:56–61; Mark 16:1–10; John 20:1–19, Luke 24:10.
11. Luke 7:36–50; Matt. 26:6–13; Mark 14:3–9; John 12:3–7.

Luke. Hence, Saint John would be identifying Mary of Bethany with the repentant sinner.

Thus, there would have been two anointings, at different times and places, but carried out by the same woman. This argument is reinforced by the fact that the four Evangelists present the same moral and psychological profile of the woman, making it difficult to visualize two different people.

MAGDALENE, FROM WHOM
SEVEN DEMONS WERE EXPELLED

As stated above, Saint John, before narrating the second anointing, says that the sister of Lazarus was the one who anointed the feet of Christ and wiped them dry with her hair. Fr. Cornelius à Lapide argues that if the repentant sinner Saint Luke refers to was not the same sister of Lazarus, Saint John should have clearly distinguished between the two so as to avoid confusion in such an important matter.[13] And Alcuin comments that, as there were many Marys among the pious women who followed Jesus, Saint John, in order to clearly identify the sister of Lazarus, mentions her most noteworthy action, that is, the anointing previously narrated by Saint Luke. This is also the opinion of Saint Augustine.[14]

For his part, soon after recounting the case of the repentant sinner, Saint Luke mentions Saint Mary Magdalene among the pious women who followed Our Lord and the Apostles to serve them and clarifies that seven devils were expelled from her.[15] Although he does not establish a link between the sinner and Saint Mary Magdalene, this is thought to be a discreet way of implying that she was the sinner who had just been mentioned.

The fact that seven devils were expelled from her is said to

---

12. John 11:2.
13. Cornelius à Lapide, p. 121.
14. Cited by St. Thomas Aquinas, *Catena Aurea in Ioannem*, Chapters 5–11, http://www.corpusthomisticum.org/cjo05.html.

further reinforce that supposition. For while it is certain that diabolical possession can be permitted by God as a trial without the person's guilt, God can also allow it, as Saint Bonaventure says, "be it as a punishment for sin, be it to correct the sinner."[16]

Starting from these leads, Saints Augustine, Cyprian, Gregory the Great, Bernard, Bernardine of Siena, Alphonsus Liguori and many others have understood that the repentant sinner, Saint Mary Magdalene and Mary the sister of Lazarus were one and the same person.[17]

Many problems remain unsolved, such as the fact that Magdala is in Galilee and Bethany is in Judea. However, Fr. H. Lesêtre says:

> The difficulties found in evangelical texts are not insuperable, and bearing in mind above all the sameness of characters, one has the right to affirm as probable that the three Marys are but one and the same person.[18]

For his part, Fr. Cornelius à Lapide says that, by her family, Mary could be from Judea (Bethany) but actually lived in Galilee (Magdala) by reason of marriage or because she possessed there a property received as inheritance.[19]

However, as we have said, the data provided by the Evangelists are not sufficient to solve all the mysteries involving the narratives about Saint Mary Magdalene.

---

15. Luke 8:2.
16. Quoted in Lucien Roure, s.v. "Possession Diabolique," *Dictionnaire de Théologie Catholique*, Vol. 12, col. 2644.
17. H. Lesêtre, s.v. "Marie Madeleine," *Dictionnaire de la Bible*, col. 814–815; Cornelius à Lapide, op. cit.; St. Alphonsus Liguori, *Obras Asceticas de San Alfonso Maria de Ligorio* (Madrid: Biblioteca de Autores Cristianos, 1952), pp. 129–131.
18. H. Lesêtre, col. 817.
19. Cornelius à Lapide, p. 121.

A GREAT SAINT, NOT A GODDESS

No reliable information is available about the life of Saint Mary Magdalene after the Resurrection of Our Lord, His Ascension into heaven and the subsequent dispersion of the Apostles to preach the Gospel. According to a pious tradition, Saint Mary Magdalene, together with Saint Lazarus, moved to what is now France to evangelize the southern part of that country. Other traditions more common in the East suggest she died in Ephesus in Asia Minor.

Be it as it may, what is certain is that the great Saint and *The Da Vinci Code*'s Gnostic feminist caricature have nothing in common.

CHAPTER 8
Divine Revelation and the
Authority of the New Testament

Without Divine Revelation, man could never know the mysteries of God that surpass the capacity of the human intellect such as the Most Blessed Trinity. On the other hand, Revelation places a divine seal of approval on other truths and principles that orient man's thought and action. Thus, the Ten Commandments make explicit and confirm the natural law written on our hearts.[1]

REVOLT AGAINST AUTHORITY

The problem of submission to authority is at the core of all religious debate.

The Catholic Church teaches that, "faith is adhesion of the intellect, under the influence of grace, to a truth revealed by God, not on account of its intrinsic evidence but on account of the authority of Him Who has revealed it."[2] And to guarantee the correct understanding of the revealed truth, Our Lord instituted a visible and unerring Church. Therefore submitting to God entails submitting to His Church, "the pillar and ground of the truth."[3]

Gnostics reject this double submission to the divine authority manifested in Revelation and in the Magisterium. They replace it with mere **knowledge** obtained directly through illumination.

In final analysis, instead of submitting, they echo Lucifer's cry: "I will not serve."[4]

---

1. Cf. Rom. 2:14.
2. Pietro Parenti, Antonio Piolanti and Salvatore Garofalo, s.v. "Faith," *Dictionary of Dogmatic Theology* (Milwaukee: The Bruce Publishing Co., 1952), p. 101.
3. 1 Tim. 3:15. "Holy Scripture and Tradition are only the remote rule of faith, while the proximate rule is the living Magisterium of the Church" (Parenti, Piolanti and Garofalo, "Magisterium of the Church," *Dictionary of Dogmatic Theology*, p. 171).
4. Jer. 2:20.

GNOSTIC "CHRISTIAN" LITERATURE

They also seek to replace the Christian Gospels with their own "gospels," leading Fr. Jules Lebreton, S.J., to warn:

> Christian Gnostics place their revelations under the patronage of some apostle, or, often, of Mary Magdalene, who is supposed to have received them from the risen Christ before the Ascension.[5]

In fact, modern-day propagandists of Gnosticism such as Dan Brown want people to believe that Christianity is a deviation from Gnosticism, the true religion. For this end they present the Gnostic gospels as "the **earliest** Christian records" and the "**unaltered** gospels."[6]

As for their being the earliest, suffice it to say that the Gnostic "Gospel of Philip" (which Brown cites as evidence that Jesus married Mary Magdalene) mentions the Gospels of Saint Matthew and Saint Mark and Saint Paul's Epistle to the Corinthians.[7]

Comparing the age of the Gnostic texts with that of the Church's canon, Philip Jenkins, professor of History and Religious Studies at Pennsylvania State University, comments:

> While the canonical gospels were completed by 100 or so, it is unlikely that any of the Nag Hammadi materials date from much before 150, and most were probably written between 150 and 250.[8]

5. Jules Lebreton, S.J., and Jacques Zeiller, *The History of the Primitive Church* (New York: The MacMillan Co., 1944), Vol. 1, p. 356.
6. *DVC*, pp. 245, 248. (Our emphasis.)
7. James M. Robinson, ed., "The Gospel of Philip," *The Nag Hammadi Library*, pp. 143–144, 151.
8. Philip Jenkins, *Hidden Gospels* (Oxford: Oxford University Press, 2001), pp. 92–93.

In short, as Fr. William P. Saunders notes, the Church did not accept the Gnostic gospels because

- their origin could not be traced to the apostolic age and genuine apostolic authorship,
- they did not have a history of liturgical use, and
- they contained heretical teachings.[9]

CONSTANTINE AND THE CANON OF THE BIBLE

Among the absurdities in *The Da Vinci Code* is the claim that Emperor Constantine established the canon of the Bible for political ends.[10]

When Constantine became emperor in 306 there already was a general consensus (only slightly changed later) on which books were considered to be of divine inspiration.

Regarding the books of the Old Testament, two collections of texts were accepted among the Jews: the Jerusalem text in Hebrew and the Alexandrine text in Greek.

At the time of Jesus, Alexandrine texts were in use also in Palestine. For example, 300 of the 350 Old Testament citations in the New Testament refer to the Alexandrine version. For this reason the Church began to use the Alexandrine collection, also known as the Septuagint,[11] in its liturgy and homilies, thus giving origin to the canon of the Old Testament.[12]

Regarding the New Testament, a precious document called the Muratorian Canon was found in 1740. The text (presently in the Milan Library) contains the Latin translation of a Greek

---

9. Cf. Fr. William P. Saunders, "Gnostic Gospels."
10. See Chapter 3.
11. Septuagint is the name given to the translation from Hebrew to Greek by seventy Jewish scholars around 300–200 B.C. in Alexandria, Egypt. Cf. www.septuagint.net.
12. Cf. Jose Maria Bover, S.J., and Francisco Cantera Burgos, *Sagrada Biblia* (Madrid: Biblioteca de Autores Cristianos, 1961); Raymond E. Brown, S.S., and Raymond F. Collins, "Canonicity," *The New Jerome Biblical Commentary* (Englewood Cliffs, N.J.: Prentice Hall, 1990), pp. 1034–1054; F. Shroeder, s.v. "Bible III (Canon)," *The New Catholic Encyclopedia*, Vol. 2, pp. 386–396.

text written between 160 and 200.[13] The document makes very clear that the writings of the New Testament as we know them today had already been fixed by the end of the second century, except for the Epistles of Saint James and Saint Peter. Likewise the document clearly demonstrates the Christian community's rejection of the Gnostic texts of Valentinus, Metiades, Basilides and Marcion.

> But we accept nothing at all of Arsinoes, or Valentinus, or Metiades. Those also [are rejected] who composed a new book of Psalms for Marcion together with Basilides and the Cataphrygians of Asia.[14]

F. Shroeder affirms in the *New Catholic Encyclopedia*:

> At the beginning of the third century the New Testament canon had passed the first major step toward fixation. Further doubts would center on other than the Gospels and the main Pauline corpus.[15]

In face of the polemics of the sixteenth century, when Luther and other innovators rejected several books of the Bible (or parts of those books), the Council of Trent dogmatically defined the canon of the Bible in respect to both the Old and

---

13. "The date of composition is clear from lines 74–77: 'Very recently, in our times, Hermas wrote the *Shephard*, when his brother, Bishop Pius, was sitting in the chair of the Church of the City of Rome.' The pontificate of Pius I was about A.D. 142–155." W. G. Most, s.v. "Muratorian Canon," *The New Catholic Encyclopedia*, Vol. 10, p. 81.
14. "The Muratorian Canon," *Early Christian Writings*, www.earlychristianwritings.com/text/muratorian-latin.html. Cf. J. P. Kirsch, s.v. "Muratorian Canon," *The Catholic Encyclopedia*, www.newadvent.org/cathen/10642a.htm; and Henri Daniel-Rops, *What is the Bible?* (New York: Hawthorn Books, 1959), p. 35.
15. F. Shroeder, s.v. "Bible III," *The New Catholic Encyclopedia*, Vol. 2, p. 394.

New Testaments.[16]

THE COUNCIL OF NICEA
AND THE "PAGAN" EMPEROR

Brown refers to Emperor Constantine as a "pagan" and finds it ironic that a pagan made the Christian Bible and turned Jesus into God at the Council of Nicea.[17]

The conversion of Constantine to Christianity is a fact attested to by historians of the time (Lactantius and Eusebius of Cesarea). Moreover, after much controversy, modern critics have accepted the fact as well.

In his book *Constantine The Great*, Lloyd B. Holsapple comments on the aftermath of the emperor's miraculous victory at the Battle of Milvian Bridge when he invoked the God of Christians.

> This conversion did not mean necessarily a complete inward moral reformation. It did not involve a full understanding of the content of the Christian revelation. But it did mean that he had publicly declared for the Christians' God, and from that declaration he would never recede.... Although he was not baptized until he realized the approach of death, though he did not even become a catechumen, the problems of the Christians and their welfare were his primary concern.[18]

Fr. Francis Murphy, C.S.S.R., likewise says:

> The religious convictions of Constantine have been the object of numerous controversies. His con-

---

16. Ibid., p. 395.
17. *DVC*, pp. 231, 233.
18. Lloyd B. Holsapple, *Constantine the Great* (New York: Sheed & Ward, 1942), pp. 175–176.

version to Christianity in 312 is now almost universally acknowledged, although the quality of his adherence to the Christian faith is still disputed. That he postponed Baptism until his deathbed is no criterion, for the practice was common, and he later insisted that he had hoped to be baptized in the Jordan.[19]

Advised by a confessor of the Faith, Hosius of Cordova,[20] Constantine convened a meeting of the bishops at Nicea to discuss the great problem of the moment: the spread of the Arian heresy. Obviously, that council would have no value, nor would it be counted among the Church's Ecumenical Councils, had Constantine's convocation or the participating bishops' decisions not been approved by Pope Saint Sylvester I.

What was the Arian heresy? A "Christianized" version of Gnosticism. The *Dictionary of Dogmatic Theology* thus summarizes the main errors of Arianism:

> Chief points of this heresy are:
>
> **a)** The one true God is **not generated** and is not communicable to creatures.
>
> **b)** In order to create the world God generated the **Word**, who, since He had a beginning, is not God, but an **intermediary** being, between God and the world.
>
> **c)** The substance of the Word, therefore, is **different** from the substance of God (the Father). He is called **Son** of the Father, not in the proper and natural sense, but in the sense

---

19. F.X. Murphy, s.v. "Constantine I, The Great, Roman Emperor," *The Catholic Encyclopedia*, Vol. 4, p. 226.

20. "The foremost Western champion of orthodoxy in the early anti–Arian struggle; born about 256; died about 358, either at Sirmium or in Spain" (Edward Myers, s.v. "Hosius of Cordova," *The Catholic Encyclopedia*, Vol. 7, p. 475).

of **adopted** son.

Arius evidently draws the elements of his heresy a bit from Gnosticism.[21]

The Council of Nicea was held in 325 with the participation of bishops and theologians of great renown, including Saint Athanasius. At his bidding the council condemned the Arian heresy and proclaimed the Symbol (or Creed) of Nicea, a complete refutation of Gnosticism:

> We believe in one God the Father Almighty, Maker of all things visible and invisible; and in one Lord Jesus Christ, the only begotten of the Father, that is, of the substance [ek tes ousias] of the Father, God of God, light of light, true God of true God, begotten not made, of the same substance with the Father [homoousion to patri], through whom all things were made both in heaven and on earth; who for us men and our salvation descended, was incarnate, and was made man, suffered and rose again the third day, ascended into heaven and cometh to judge the living and the dead. And in the Holy Ghost. Those who say: There was a time when He was not, and He was not before He was begotten; and that He was made out of nothing (ex ouk onton); or who maintain that He is of another hypostasis or another substance [than the Father], or that the Son of God is created, or mutable, or subject to change, [them] the Catholic Church anathematizes.[22]

21. Parenti, Piolanti and Garofalo, "Arianism," p. 20. (Emphasis in the original.)
22. H. Leclercq, s.v. "The First Council of Nicaea," *The Catholic Encyclopedia*, Vol. 11, p. 45.

THE BIBLE, A HEAVEN-SENT TREASURE

There is no better way to end these considerations than to cite these beautiful words of Pope Pius XII about the Sacred Scriptures:

> Inspired by the Divine Spirit, the Sacred Writers composed those books, which God, in His paternal charity towards the human race, deigned to bestow on them in order "to teach, to reprove, to correct, to instruct in justice: that the man of God may be perfect, furnished to every good work." (2 Tim. 3:16–17) This heaven-sent treasure Holy Church considers as the most precious source of doctrine on faith and morals. No wonder therefore that, as she received it intact from the hands of the Apostles, so she kept it with all care, defended it from every false and perverse interpretation and used it diligently as an instrument for securing the eternal salvation of souls, as almost countless documents in every age strikingly bear witness.[23]

True Gospels and Gnostic Gospels

NAG HAMMADI AND THE GNOSTIC GOSPELS

Modern Gnosticism benefited greatly when fifty-two ancient texts were found buried in an earthenware jar near the Egyptian town of Nag Hammadi in 1945. Translations proliferated and Gnostics quickly claimed that the mysterious writings were actually the true gospels that had been suppressed by leaders of the early Church. Often called the

---

23. Pius XII, Encyclical *Divino Afflante Spiritu*, in Claudia Carlen, I.H.M., *The Papal Encyclicals 1939–1958* (New York: McGrath Publishing Co., 1981), no. 1.

secret or hidden gospels, they are in fact neither. Only five have the name "gospel" attached to them and they in no way resemble the richness and historicity of their four counterparts in the New Testament.

Many Church Fathers, of which Saint Irenaeus (125–203) is the best example, wrote volumes refuting the writings of the Gnostics of the mid-second century whom they quite correctly saw as subverting the beliefs established by Christ and the Apostles.

The texts found at Nag Hammadi are either based on earlier heresies or are Coptic translations of them. Since the oldest text did not appear until around 150 A.D., we are not talking about two systems that developed side by side as the Gnostics would have it.

The organized, monolithic, hierarchical Church predated these writings by several decades, perhaps even a hundred years. Therefore the so-called hidden gospels represent the effort of a group of dissidents and malcontents bent on subverting the traditional beliefs established by Divine Revelation.

THE AUTHENTICITY OF
THE NEW TESTAMENT GOSPELS

When the enemies of Christian tradition sow confusion and doubt about the authorship of the four Gospels, they reveal their ignorance of the existing documentation. Numerous ante-Nicene authors such as Saint Irenaeus of Lyons (125–203), Tertullian of Carthage (150–220) and Origen of Alexandria (185–254) not only list the four evangelists but give supplementary information that adds to our understanding of the purpose and circumstances of their composition.

The Apostle Matthew originally wrote his Gospel in

Hebrew hoping to induce the Jews to accept Christianity. The followers of Saint Peter in Rome prevailed on his pupil Mark to leave them a written account of Peter's oral teaching. Luke, a Greek-speaking gentile, wrote about the truths he had learned during his many journeys with Saint Paul. John, "the disciple Jesus loved," wrote his Gospel in Ephesus to crush the errors of the growing Gnostic movement that denied the Divinity of Christ.

The first two Gospels can be dated only to the closest decade. Saint Matthew's Hebrew text was written between 40 and 50 A.D. and the Greek translation followed approximately ten years later. All the evidence indicates Saint Mark's Gospel was composed during the period 53–63 A.D. Saint Luke's Gospel coincides with Saint Paul's first Roman imprisonment in the years 61–63. Saint John's Gospel has traditionally been assigned to the year 100.

The diffusion and integrity of the Gospels can be proven by comparing the quotations from the New Testament of Irenaeus, Tertullian and Clement of Alexandria (150–215). Irenaeus quotes the New Testament 1,819 times, Clement 2,406 times, and Tertullian an incredible total of 7,259 times. A comparison of these texts with each other and the New Testament as it exists today shows that the readings are essentially the same. Since over 4,000 very old manuscripts or fragments exist we can say that there is more manuscript evidence for the Gospels than for any of the ancient Latin or Greek classics.[24]

24. Jeremias Wells, "Gnosticism, Anti-Catholicism and *The Da Vinci Code*," *Crusade*, Nov.-Dec. 2004, p. 14.

CHAPTER 9
The Knights Templar

As already mentioned, Brown bases *The Da Vinci Code* on works like *Holy Blood, Holy Grail* and *The Templar Revelation* that falsify the history of the Knights Templar.

THE TEMPLARS' REAL SECRET: RELIGIOUS FERVOR AND MARTIAL PROWESS

To explain the prestige and power of the Knights Templar one need not resort to outlandish conspiracy theories or gratuitous conjectures. It suffices to know the history and psychology of medieval man. As Charles Moeller aptly notes: "The order owed its rapid growth in popularity to the fact that it combined the two great passions of the Middle Ages, religious fervor and martial prowess."[1]

As often happens in great institutions, the origins of the Knights Templar were very modest and almost accidental.

Though the Crusaders conquered Jerusalem in 1099, the roads leading to the Holy City continued to be constantly attacked by Muslims. Christian pilgrims traveled at great risk. In 1118, Hugues de Payens, a French knight from the family of the counts of Champagne, and some of his friends decided to consecrate their lives to protect those roads. So began the Order of the Poor Knights of Christ—one of the glories of Christian civilization.

Thanks to the influence of Saint Bernard of Clairvaux, the nascent order was approved by the Council of Troyes in 1128. Baldwin II, King of Jerusalem, granted them part of his palace adjoining the ruins of the Temple of Solomon. They therefore became popularly known as the Poor Knights of the Temple.

The great abbot of Clairvaux wrote one of the most beautiful pages in Christian literature outlining the profile and mission

---

1. Charles Moeller, s.v. "The Knights Templars," *The Catholic Encyclopedia*, Vol. 14, pp. 493–495.

of the monk-soldiers: *In Praise of the New Knighthood (Liber ad milites Templi: De laude novae militiae)*.[2]

This was the first of the Religious Orders of Chivalry, which united the virtues of religious and military life. In addition to the three classical vows—poverty, obedience and chastity—knights made the crusader's vow, that is, to combat the infidels with armed force.

The beauty of this ideal and the support of Saint Bernard—the greatest religious figure of the time—caused the new militia to grow quickly. Over the years the order received donations and legacies from great benefactors, assuring its material survival.

As the order grew, its castle-monasteries multiplied throughout western Europe and the Middle East. To avoid robberies and other property losses on major trips, travelers turned to the Templars. A pilgrim could deposit money at a convent in France or England and receive a voucher authorizing him to withdraw the same amount at his destination in Cyprus or Jerusalem. Due to the different exchange rates that normally existed between the two points, the Order generally profited from these transactions.

The Knights Templar inspired such trust that kings confided their royal treasuries to their custody. As their patrimony grew, the Templars also started to make bank-style loans.[3] From the profits, the Order financed its military activities, which required huge sums.

THE PRICE OF BLOOD

More than gold and silver, the Templars' heroic defense of the Holy Land cost them a high price in blood. In two centuries of combat against Muslims, about 20,000 soldier-monks perished on the battlefield or were executed by the enemy after

---

2. See www.the-orb.net/encyclop/religion/monastic/bernard.html.
3. Cf. Jacques Wolff, "La chute des moines banquiers," *Historia*, Feb. 1995, pp. 18–21.

being taken prisoner. Unlike other knights, the Templars were forbidden by their rule to pay ransom. Since the enemy could gain no profit from his prisoner, the options for a captured Knight Templar were denial of the Catholic faith or death. Martyrdom was the norm.[4]

DECADENCE OF THE MIDDLE AGES

In 1285, Philip IV, called the Fair, became king of France. He was the very opposite of his grandfather, Saint Louis IX. While his grandfather represented the spirit of chivalry in what it had of most sublime—heroism at the service of the Faith—the grandson displayed cynicism and pragmatism and hunger for power and riches. He surrounded himself with legists—specialists in Roman Law who eventually transformed the organic monarchy of the Middle Ages into the absolutist monarchy of the Renaissance.

When "the two great passions of the Middle Ages, religious fervor and martial prowess," began to decline, they were replaced with a practical and selfish mentality. The popularity of the Templars as well as the Crusades waned. In many places the fervor of the soldier-monks themselves declined.

With the fall of the Christian Kingdom of Outremer (the Kingdom Beyond the Sea) in 1291,[5] many began to question the Order's very *raison d'être* and to covet its goods.

---

4. Cf. Moeller, s.v. "The Knights Templars," *The Catholic Encyclopedia.*
5. Acre, the Kingdom of Outremer's capital after Saladin conquered Jerusalem, fell to the Mameluke sultan Al-Ashraf Khalil on May 28, 1291. By July 31 the sultan had taken the five remaining Christian strongholds in the Holy Land and the Kingdom of Outremer was no more. Hoping to regain a foothold on the mainland, the Templars continued to resist from the waterless island of Ruad, two miles from their fallen city-fortress of Tortosa. However, in September 1303 – while Philip the Fair's emissaries slapped Pope Boniface VIII in Agnani – the Templars evacuated the island and fell back to Cyprus. Cf. Stephen Howarth, *The Knights Templar* (New York: Dorset Press, 1982).

PHILIP IV DECLARES HIS ASCENDANCY OVER THE POPE

The Templars soon became involved in a tragedy that was an extension of the struggle of Philip the Fair to impose his tutelage on the papacy and the Church.

In 1296, Philip began to fall out with Pope Boniface VIII. This great Pontiff courageously resisted the French king's interference in French Church matters. In 1302 he published the Bull *Unam Sanctam*. It affirmed that the spiritual power has a mission to inspire, guide and correct temporal power, without absorbing it, and that both powers should work in harmony for the good of the people and of souls.

The king and his legists reacted by calumniating the Pope. Parliament was convened and the legist Guillaume de Nogaret accused the Pope of heresy, simony, witchcraft and sodomy, the same charges he would later level at the Templars.

This conflict gave rise to a scene that many regard as symbolic of the end of the Middle Ages. French troops invaded the castle of Anagni near Rome where the Pope had taken refuge. Nogaret insulted the Pope, and Sciarra Colonna, a Roman patrician who was a personal enemy of the Pope and an ally of the French, slapped the Pope with an iron gauntlet. The 86-year-old Pontiff, weakened by this great offense and brutality, died shortly thereafter (October 1303).

After the very short reign of Benedict XI, Philip the Fair weighed heavily in the election of a French Pope, Bertrand de Got, Archbishop of Bordeaux, who took the name Clement V and transferred Church government to Avignon in France.[6]

KING PHILIP IV MOVES AGAINST THE TEMPLARS

Having subjected the papacy, the French king turned against

---

6. Cf. Ivan Gobry, "Comment le Roi de France soumit la Papauté," *Historia*, Feb. 1995, no. 578, pp. 12–17; Moeller, s.v. "The Knights Templars," *The Catholic Encyclopedia*.

the Templars, the most visible symbol of medieval Catholic combativeness. Pierre Vial, professor of Medieval History at Lyon University, writes:

> The smear mechanism unleashed against the Templars utilizes the same methods, accusations and murderous words used in the past against illustrious adversaries of Philip the Fair: Bishop Bernard Saisset and Pope Boniface VIII.[7]

During the night of Friday, October 13, 1307, in an unprecedented police action, armed troops invaded every Templar castle-monastery in France. The Templars offered no resistance to the king's warrant for their arrest.

The knights were interrogated under brutal torture. Forty knights died during questioning. A large number, however, to save themselves from further torment made the confessions their executioners wanted to hear. The Grand Master himself, Jacques de Molay, admitted his "guilt."

A statement by Knight Templar Ponsar de Gisy after he confessed under torture is revealing:

> If they subject me once again to the same torture I will say anything they want! Though I'm ready to give up my life and be burned or boiled for the Order's honor, on the condition that the suffering be brief, I am unable to bear long torments like the ones they [the royal inquisitors] put me through.[8]

Pope Clement V protested such proceedings, but the king threatened him with reprisals. As in the time of Boniface VIII,

---

7. Pierre Vial, "L'Arrestation Spetaculaire des Templiers: Etaient-ils innocents ou coupables?" *Historia*, Feb. 1995, p. 25.
8. Ibid., p. 28.

"virulent libels began to circulate accusing the Pope of favoring heresy and heretics. Clement V is unable to resist these pressures."[9]

The Templars who recanted their confessions were condemned by the king-controlled Inquisition and burned alive as relapsed heretics. The Grand Master was among them. While being burnt at the stake close to Notre Dame Cathedral in Paris, he called God as his witness that the Order was innocent and solemnly convoked both king and Pope to the judgment seat of God. Both died within the year.

The weak French Pope opened his own investigation of the Order. According to Charles Moeller,

> The culpability of single persons, which was looked upon as established, did not involve the guilt of the order. Although the defense of the order was poorly conducted, it could not be proved that the order as a body professed any heretical doctrine, or that a secret rule, distinct from the official rule, was practiced. Consequently, at the General Council of Vienne in Dauphiné, on 16 October, 1311, the majority were favorable to the maintenance of the order. The pope, irresolute and harassed, finally adopted a middle course: he decreed the dissolution, not the condemnation of the order, and not by penal sentence, but by an Apostolic Decree (Bull of March 22, 1312).[10]

The kings of Portugal and Aragon perceived the injustice of this decree and petitioned the Pope to establish new orders of chivalry for the Knights Templar in their realms. Thus, with papal approval, the king of Portugal created the Order of

---

9. Ibid., p. 28.
10. Moeller, s.v. "The Knights Templars," *The Catholic Encyclopedia.*

Christ, which in the following century spearheaded the conquest of the seas, extending Christianity to lands until then unknown; in Aragon the king created the Order of Montesa to defend Christian territories from attacks by Moors and pirates.

In other countries, the Templars' property was given to the Knights of St. John of Jerusalem (later known as the Knights of Malta). Most of the remaining knights joined this or other orders of chivalry (the Teutonic Knights, the Knights of Calatrava, and so on). Others returned to civilian life.

The Poor Knights of Christ of the Temple of Jerusalem were never restored as an order by the Church. Regardless of their goals, all groups and associations claiming to be a continuation of the Knights Templar lack legitimacy.

Dubious Accusations Against the Templar Order

Using common sense arguments, Professor Alan Forey, a specialist in military orders, casts doubt on the accusations against the Templars:

a) Though all the Order's convents were raided on the same night, no idol or trace of any secret ceremony was found.

b) Throughout the Order's history many knights returned to civilian life, but none of these knights denounced the Order's "idolatry."

c) It would have been practically impossible to hide the Order's "anti-Christian character" for so long.

d) The authorities obtained admissions of guilt only by torture; these were often recanted.[11]

---

11. Cf. Alan Forey, "The Military Orders," *The Oxford Illustrated History of the Crusades* (New York: Oxford University Press, 1995), p. 215.

CHAPTER 10
The Priory of Sion: A Fiction of Mythomaniacs and Forgers

As for Brown's Priory of Sion, its role and importance is pure fiction—a fabrication of mythomaniacs and forgers.

For starters, the claim that the Priory's supposed founder, Godfrey of Bouillon, son of Eustace II, Count of Boulogne and Ida, daughter of Godfrey, Duke of Lower Lorraine, was a descendant of Our Lord, besides being blasphemous, is so outrageous that it defies the imagination. Also, the great leader of the First Crusade never founded any secret society, let alone the Priory of Sion. On this point we have the testimony of history.

Furthermore, there is a chronological impossibility. Godfrey was born around 1060 and died in 1100. The Priory of Sion was founded in the twentieth century, in 1956 to be precise, by a mythomaniac called Pierre Plantard. The Priory has nothing to do with the Holy Land. The Mount Sion it is named after is a small hill outside St. Julien-en-Genevois in France, where Plantard registered his association.[1]

Dan Brown claims Pierre Plantard descended from the Merovingians (something Plantard himself began to claim at a certain point of his disturbed life) and from Jesus and Mary Magdalene (something Plantard allowed others to say about him, but later denied). Brown's claim that Plantard lived in hiding for fear of the Church is also false.[2]

Actually, Pierre-Athanase-Marie Plantard (1920–2000), son of a valet and a concierge, was a misfit, living off small chores and trying to build a myth for himself. On February 13, 2004,

---

1. Cf. http://priory-of-sion.com. This web site offers abundant first-hand documentation about this pseudo-priory.
2. Cf. *DVC*, pp. 260, 442; Massimo Introvigne, "Beyond *The Da Vinci Code*: History and Myth of the Priory of Sion," June, 2005, http://www.cesnur.org/2005/pa_introvigne.htm.

The Abbey—not Priory— of Mount Sion

The Crusaders rebuilt the Church of Mount Sion in Jerusalem, which was in ruins. Placed under the care of the Canons of St. Augustine (also known as Austen Canons), it became the Abbey of Mount Sion. It has nothing in common with Dan Brown's Priory of Sion. After the fall of the Christian Kingdom the monks relocated to Orleans in France. In 1619 the community ceased to exist and King Louis XIII transferred its property to the Jesuits.[3]

---

3. Cf. A. Allaria, s.v. "Canons and Canonesses Regular," *The Catholic Encyclopedia*, Vol. 3, p. 288–297; Bernard Hamilton, "Truth and Falsity in *The Da Vinci Code*," *The Times Literary Supplement*, Jun. 8, 2005, www.the-tls.co.uk/this_week/story.aspx?story_id=2111067.

Claude Charlot, head of the Paris Police Archives and Museum, wrote the following in response to an information request from English researcher Paul Smith:

> About Pierre Plantard, alias "Pierre de France" or "Varrau de Verrestra," we have on file a small folder under reference #GA P7. This folder, with about forty pages, essentially exposes the activity of Pierre Plantard during the Occupation....
>
> Pierre Plantard appeared to be an illuminated young man, regularly discovering hypothetical "Jewish-Masonic" conspiracies and continuously offering people his services without receiving the least attention. His political weight was nonexistent, his influence nil.
>
> It seems that he spent his time creating more or

less fictitious movements (French National Renewal; Catholic Youth Group) and sulphurous programs ("Purge and Renewal of France"); he wrote some bulletins without repercussion (Rénovation Française, Vaincre); and he falsely boasted of being friends with politicians to make himself important.[4]

A FORGED DOSSIER
PLANTED IN THE NATIONAL LIBRARY

Dan Brown refers to an "important document" discovered by the Bibliothèque Nationale titled *Les Dossiers Secrets*. It is listed as number 4° lm1 249.[5]

The document is a forgery and was planted in France's national library. To give credibility to his wild genealogical claims and his meaningless Priory of Sion, Plantard enlisted the help of a ruined Belgian marquis, Philippe de Chérisey (1925–1985). Together, the two forged several documents and deposited them in the Bibliothèque Nationale in Paris between 1965 and 1967.

Using these false documents, a third accomplice, Gérard de Sède (1921–2004), a specialist in esoteric topics, wrote and published *L'Or de Rennes* in 1967, which made Pierre Plantard's imaginings famous.[6] On this book are based a series of others that pile absurdity upon absurdity. The authors of *Holy Blood, Holy Grail* added to the confusion with the state-

---

4. Letter from Claude Charlot on Feb. 13, 2004, French fac-simile at http://priory-of-sion.com/psp/gap/cletter.html. See also http://priory-of-sion.com/psp/id170.html.

5. Cf. *DVC*, pp. 206 and 326.

6. Cf. Massimo Introvigne, "Beyond *The Da Vinci Code*: History and Myth of the Priory of Sion"; Gérard de Sède, *Rennes-le-Chateau – le dossier, les impostures, les phantasmes, les hypothèse* (Paris: Editions Robert Laffont, 1988), pp. 107–111; "Priory of Sion Parchments and Steven Mizrach," http://priory-of-sion.com/posd/parchments.html; Wieland Willker, "Codex Bezae and the Da Vinci Code: A Textcritical Look at the Rennes-le-Chateau Hoax," http://www-user.uni-bremen.de/~wie/Rennes/.

ment that Plantard, in addition to descending from the Merovingians, was of the line of Jesus and Mary Magdalene.[7]

Regarding these documents, Aviad Kleinberg, professor of History at Tel Aviv University, notes:

> The national library in Paris, like the Jewish National and University Library in Jerusalem and the Library of Congress, does hold such documents. It is not responsible for their contents or quality.[8]

On the imaginings contained in *The Da Vinci Code*, the same professor comments:

> What is correct in this tale? Hardly anything. Brown's main contentions are taken from a series of forgeries that were concocted in France in the 1930s and 1940s by a group of believers in esoteric doctrines, extreme leftists, anti-Semites and supporters of Petain. This nonsense later garnered publicity and was circulated in a number of books, the best-known of which is "Holy Blood, Holy Grail," which was published in the 1980s and was hugely successful. All of these forgeries (about the Priory of Sion and the spurious list of its heads) were exposed long ago, including the dossiers secrets, which Brown mentions as authentic documents from the Bibliotheque Nationale in Paris.[9]

---

7. Cf. Baigent, Leigh and Lincoln, passim.
8. Aviad Kleinberg, "The Feminist Mystique."
9. Ibid.

PART III

The Code Behind the Code
Gnosticism: Doctrine and History

CHAPTER 11
Gnosticism: The Devil's False Wisdom

*"For this is not wisdom, descending
from above: but earthly, sensual, devilish."*
— James 3:15

According to Catholic doctrine, God is infinite and therefore has in Himself all possible perfection; he suffices unto Himself for His eternal happiness. Nothing required that He create the universe therefore.

However, good is diffusive. And since God is the Supreme Good and almighty, He spread His goodness by creating. In a totally gratuitous act of love, God brought forth the universe and everything in it from nothing.

A reflection of the divine perfection, Creation renders extrinsic glory to God: "The heavens shew forth the glory of God, and the firmament declareth the work of his hands."[1]

LOVE FOR LOVE
God endowed His angelic and human creatures with free will, so they could choose to love Him. Having been given the inestimable gift of existence out of love, these creatures ought to reciprocate with gratitude and submission.

REVOLT AGAINST THE BENEFACTOR
Instead, some angels, admiring their own perfection in a disorderly fashion, proudly thought: "I will be like the most High."[2] Misusing their free will, they refused God a loving submission. Hence Lucifer's cry of revolt: "I will not serve."[3]

---

1. Ps. 18:2.
2. Isaias 14:14. Here the Prophet refers to the king of Babylon. Some Fathers of the Church apply this passage to the devil.
3. Jer. 2:20. This too is an allegorical and spiritual rather than strictly exegetical application.

Creation: An Expression of God's Goodness

"God, by His goodness and omnipotent power, not to increase His own beatitude, and not to add to, but to manifest His perfection by the blessings which He bestows on creatures, with most free volition, immediately from the beginning of time fashioned each creature out of nothing, spiritual and corporeal, namely angelic and mundane."[4]

---

4. First Vatican Council, *Dogmatic Constitution Concerning Catholic Faith*, Denzinger, no. 1783.

These rebellious angels were expelled from Heaven and cast into the abyss by Saint Michael the Archangel and his legions.[5] Our Lord Himself mentioned this defeat of Satan when He told His disciples: "I saw Satan like lightning falling from heaven."[6]

In the Garden of Eden, Satan, the deceiver, the enemy of mankind, tempted our first parents to the sin of pride that had led to his own downfall: "to be like the Most High." He incited Eve to disobey the Creator as a way of becoming equal to Him: "You shall be as Gods."[7] Since then he has unceasingly tempted mankind with his "earthly, sensual, devilish" wisdom.[8]

GNOSTICISM: THE DEVIL'S WISDOM

Gnosis (knowledge in Greek), or Gnosticism, is a set of

---

5. Apoc. 12:7–9.
6. Luke 10:18.
7. Gen. 3:5.
8. James 3:15. As St. Paul says, "Now the Spirit manifestly saith that in the last times some shall depart from the faith, giving heed to spirits of error and doctrines of devils. Speaking lies in hypocrisy and having their conscience seared. Forbidding to marry, to abstain from meats, which God hath created to be received with thanksgiving by the faithful and by them that have known the truth" (1 Tim. 4:1–3).

doctrines and practices by which the devil tempts man to join his frustrated bid to be like God.

How can his absurd proposition even seem plausible, since it is opposed to our perception of ourselves and of the created universe? How can there be parity between a finite and mortal creature and the infinite and eternal God? How to destroy in man his natural sense of gratitude and submission to God, to whom he owes not only existence but also preservation and elevation to the state of grace and Redemption?

To place creature and Creator on the same level, one must deny the fundamental difference between them. One must make believe that creature and Creator are equal in nature and that the creation of the universe is not due to a free act of love on God's part.

A TRUTH KNOWN ONLY TO THE ENLIGHTENED

Thus, Gnosticism—"earthly, sensual, devilish" wisdom—invents myths to explain divine nature and human nature, creation and salvation. These myths run contrary not only to Divine Revelation and wholesome philosophical principles but human experience itself.

Gnostic systems promote a new dimension of reality off limits to common mortals and known only to those who receive the illuminations of Gnosis. It is a magic knowledge distinct from knowledge through reason that transforms its possessor into what Gnostics call a different, perfect, or spiritual (pneumatic) being.

Like everything based on falsehood, Gnostic myths and theories are full of internal contradictions and veiled in obscure and complicated language. They involve a dizzying array of beings and names. The resulting confusion is at times mistaken for profoundness.

THE GNOSTIC MYTH

The multifaceted aspect of Gnosticism makes a synthesis difficult. However here are the main points:[9]

1. Dualism: God versus Matter

- God is a totally inaccessible being in no way connected to the creation of the visible universe or the destiny of man; He is inaccessible and unknowable to the point that some Gnostics call him the "Not-Being."[10]
- In opposition to God, also existing eternally, is Matter, which is the principle of evil (dualism).
- God emanated numberless divine, supra-mundane Æons, decreasingly perfect, which, taken all together, constitute the fullness (*pleroma*) of Divine life. These Aeons are bisexual, androgynous, or form pairs with their counterparts (*Syzygies*).
- The last of these Æons, High Sophia (Wisdom), produced an inferior Sophia (also named Achamoth), responsible for the material world.

2. Creation, the Work of an Evil God

- The inferior Sophia ("sacred feminine"), having indulged in a desire to know the Unknowable God, was

---

9. For a deeper study, see "Gnosticism," in *The Catholic Encyclopedia*, Vol. 6, pp. 592–602, and also the entries for "Aeons," "Demiurge," "Antinomianism," "Nicolaites" and "Albingenses." Also useful, and less technical, is "Gnosticism," in *The New Catholic Encyclopedia*, Vol. 6, p. 523–528, and "Jewish Gnosticism," pp. 528–533. See also Hans Jonas, "Gnosticism," in *The Encyclopedia of Philosophy* (New York: The MacMillan Co. & The Free Press, 1967), Vol. 3, pp. 336–342. A more complete study by the same author is *The Gnostic Religion*. On the struggle of the early Church against Gnosticism and for a good exposition on the various Gnostic heresies of the time, see Jules Lebreton, S.J., and Jacques Zeiller, *The History of the Primitive Church*, Vol. 1, pp. 355–359, Vol. 2, pp. 617–715.

10. Thus, the Gnostic heretic Basilides (second century A.D.) affirms: "God is Not-Being, even He, who made the world out of what was not; Not-Being made Not-Being." J.P. Arendzen, s.v. "Basilides," *The Catholic Encyclopedia*, Vol. 2, p. 327.

expelled from the Pleroma.

- In a bid to reproduce, she became androgynous (bisexual)[11] and through self-fecundation conceived and gave birth to an abortive, distorted and evil being called the *Demiurge* (Craftsman, Maker).
- This abortive being, unaware of his divine origin, of the sublime reality of the Pleroma, and of the existence of the Inaccessible God, believed he himself was the only God.
- Endowed with the powers of his mother, Sophia, the Demiurge went on to create the visible universe, shaping eternal Matter to this end.
- Thus, the creation of the visible universe is not a work of God or the result of a free act of love, but comes from an evil being, the Demiurge (who Gnostics identify with the God of the Old Testament).

3. A Divine Particle Imprisoned in Man

- For reasons that vary according to each Gnostic system, a divine spark either fell or was mistakenly attracted to the inferior regions, becoming imprisoned in matter.
- Making use of this matter containing the divine particle, the Demiurge and his aides, the *Archontes* (Rulers), created man.
- Man is, then, composed of three distinct elements: the material body, an immaterial soul dominated however by matter (the psyche) and the spirit (pneuma), the divine particle.

4. Messenger Instead of Redeemer

- The semi-divinities residing in the Pleroma decided to rescue the divine particle imprisoned in man.
- For this end they sent a Messenger or Illuminator whose

---

11. See Chapter 4.

role was to reveal to man, through an *illumination* or *superior knowledge* (Gnosis), his true nature since, because of the link with his material body, man had lost the notion of his divine nature.

- Thus, Gnostic revelation is not about God and His work but about man and his own divine nature: it is a self-revelation.

5. Man Redeems God

- However, to descend to the inferior regions and try to rescue the divine particle, this Messenger or Illuminator had to take on human nature (or more precisely its appearance, since he is a pure spirit)[12] and thus be subjected to exile from the Pleroma.
- Thus, to the degree that this "savior" saves man, he is himself saved, as he is able to leave his exile and return to the Pleroma. He is, therefore, a *saved savior*.[13]

6. Salvation Through Knowledge (Gnosis)

- Unlike in Christianity, man's perfection and salvation is not worked through faith and good works but through knowledge, *illumination*, Gnosis.
- Through this illumination, man enters into contact with the divine particle imprisoned within him and gradually detaches himself from the domination of matter, becoming

---

12. The Docetist heresy affirmed that Our Lord was not true God and true man, that His body was a mere appearance (*dokesis*, appearance or semblance in Greek). Cf. J.P. Arendzen, s.v. "Docetae," *The Catholic Encyclopedia*, Vol. 5, pp. 70–72.
13. "The fact that in the discharge of his task the eternal messenger must himself assume the lot of incarnation and cosmic exile, and the further fact that, at least in the Iranian variety of the myth, he is in a sense identical with those he calls – the once lost parts of his divine self – give rise to the moving idea of the 'saved savior' (*salvator salvandus*)" (Hans Jonas, s.v. "Gnosticism," *The Encyclopedia of Philosophy*, Vol. 3, p. 340).

spiritual (*pneumatic*).[14]

7. Three Categories of Men

- Gnostics divide men into three categories: a) the *hylics*,[15] totally dominated by matter (the majority); b) the *psychics*,[16] more perfect but still influenced by matter; c) the *pneumatics*,[17] the *perfect* or *spiritual* ones, to whom complete moral license is allowed.

8. Reincarnationism

- In general, Gnostics are reincarnationists. They believe successive reincarnations are necessary for the divine particle to become entirely free to return to the Pleroma.

9. Androgynism

- Several Gnostic systems present the goddess and the first man as being both masculine and feminine.
- Some of these systems believe "original sin" was a separation of the androgynous being (Adam-Eve) into two distinct beings, masculine and feminine.

Thus, Gnosticism is a total rejection of Catholic teaching on God, Creation and the Church. It is the devil's oldest, most fundamental, and oft-recurring lie.[18] To avoid being tricked with it by the Father of Lies, we must heed the advice old Tobias gave to his son: "Never suffer pride to reign in thy mind, or in thy words: for from it all perdition took its beginning."[19]

---

14. "The Gnostic Savior does not save. Gnosticism lacks the idea of atonement. There is no sin to be atoned for, except ignorance be that sin. Nor does the Savior in any sense benefit the human race by vicarious sufferings" (J. P. Arendzen, s.v. "Gnosticism," *The Catholic Encyclopedia*, Vol. 6, p. 595).
15. From the Greek *hyle*, matter.
16. From the Greek *psyche*, the soul.
17. From the Greek *pneuma*, air, spirit, breath.
18. Cf. H. Cornelis, O.P., and A. Léonard, O.P., *La Gnose Éternelle* (Paris: Librairie Arthème Fayard, 1959).
19. Tob. 4:14.

CHAPTER 12
Gnosticism: A Perversion of Morals

Do not err: Neither fornicators nor
idolaters nor adulterers: Nor the effeminate...
shall possess the kingdom of God.
— 1 Cor. 6:9–10

Gnostic ethics—like other norms of conduct—stem from a worldview. The errors of the Gnostic worldview shape its ethics, and these prove harmful to the individual and to society.

TOTAL AMORALITY

According to Gnosticism, matter is the principle of evil. Since moral evil is of the material body, the notion of personal responsibility for one's actions is eliminated. Likewise, since perfection results from a magic knowledge, an illumination leading to direct contact with divinity, there is no need for good works or virtue; knowledge suffices. Furthermore, since the divine particle within is untarnished by evil deeds, the Gnostic need have no moral restraint.

Saint Irenaeus—who learned the Faith from Saint Polycarp, disciple of Saint John the Evangelist—was the Church's main champion against the Gnostics in the second century. In his book *Adversus Haereses* (Against Heresies) he summarizes the Gnostic argument for amorality.

> Wherefore also they maintain that good works are necessary to us, for that otherwise it is impossible we should be saved. But as to themselves, they hold that they shall be entirely and undoubtedly saved, not by means of conduct, but because they are spiritual by nature. For, just as it is impossible that material substance should partake of salvation (since, indeed, they maintain that it is incapable of receiving it), so again it

is impossible that spiritual substance (by which they mean themselves) should ever come under the power of corruption, whatever the sort of actions in which they indulged. For even as gold, when submersed in filth, loses not on that account its beauty, but retains its own native qualities, the filth having no power to injure the gold, so they affirm that they cannot in any measure suffer hurt, or lose their spiritual substance, whatever the material actions in which they may be involved.[1]

This total license is to be practiced with the purpose of liberating the divine spark within, Hans Jonas explains.

This freedom, however, is more than merely permissive; its practice is bidden by metaphysical interest.... There is a positive duty to perform every kind of action, to leave no deed undone, no possibility of freedom unrealized, in order to render nature its due and exhaust its powers; only in this way can final release from the cycle of reincarnations be obtained.[2]

TWO EXTREMES: LICENTIOUSNESS AND FALSE ASCETICISM

Contempt for the material can lead Gnostics to the licentiousness mentioned or to a false asceticism, where the Gnostic condemns, for example, carnal contact or limits it to prevent procreation and the resulting proliferation of imprisoned divine particles.[3] Again Hans Jonas:

---

1. St. Irenaeus of Lyons, *Adversus Haereses*, Book I, Chap. 6, no. 2, www.newadvent.org/fathers/0103106.htm.
2. Hans Jonas, s.v. "Gnosticism," *The Encyclopedia of Philosophy*, Vol. 3, p. 340.
3. Contemporary society's systematic campaign against procreation, with its promotion of contraception, abortion and homosexuality, shows a profound affinity with Gnosis that many fail to see.

In this life, the *pneumatics*, as the possessors of gnosis called themselves, are set apart from the great mass of mankind. The immediate illumination not only makes the individual sovereign in the sphere of knowledge...but also determines the sphere of action. Generally speaking, the pneumatic morality is determined by hostility toward the world and contempt for all mundane ties. From this principle, however, two contrary conclusions could be drawn, and both found their extreme representatives: the ascetic and the libertine. The former deduces from the possession of gnosis the obligation to avoid further contamination by the world and therefore to reduce contact with it to a minimum; the latter derives from the same possession the privilege of absolute freedom.[4]

Gnostic asceticism is not to be confused with Christian asceticism. The Gnostic ascetic, like his licentious opposite, vilifies the human body, opposes the propagation of the human race and aims to destroy the link between matter and spirit. An online publication by the Institute for Gnostic Studies reads:

> The aim of the Gnostic life is liberation, not petty morality. Our focus is on returning home to the Kingdom of Light (Pleroma), not on sustaining moral standards. While the Gnostic may not totally accept the maxim that the end justifies the means, he comes awfully close....
>
> The intrusion of morality into Gnostic practice is an irritant and nuisance. Since our goal is the Pleroma, both paths are equally of value as long as they are followed to their goal. Asceticism and indul-

---

4.   Hans Jonas, *The Gnostic Religion*, p. 46.

gence are really two phases of one process, in some sense they can be seen as the negative and plus poles of the sense continuum, neither is innately morally acceptable or unacceptable. While reproduction and family values are rejected wholeheartedly by the Gnosis, beyond this requirement, the use of sexuality via asceticism or indulgence is a choice the student makes along the way.[5]

SINNING OUT OF HATRED FOR GOD

In his study on Gnosticism, J. P. Arendzen writes this about the Gnostics in the first centuries of the Church:

> As a moral law was given by the God of the Jews [the Demiurge] and opposition to the God of the Jews was a duty, the breaking of the moral law to spite its giver was considered a solemn obligation. Such a sect, called the Nicolaites, existed in Apostolic times, their principle, according to Origen, was *parachresthai te sarki* [one should abuse one's body]. Carpocrates, whom Tertullian (De animâ, xxxv) calls a magician and a fornicator, was a contemporary of Basilides. One could only escape the cosmic powers through discharging one's obligations to them by infamous conduct. To disregard all law and sink oneself into the Monad by remembering one's pre-existence in the Cosmic Unit—such was the Gnosis of Carpocrates. His son Epiphanes followed his father's doctrine so closely that he died in consequence of his sins at the age of seventeen.[6]

---

5.   http://pages.zoom.co.uk/thuban/html/dark.htm.
6.   J. P. Arendzen, s.v. "Gnosticism," *The Catholic Encyclopedia*, Vol. 6, p. 599.

SOCIETAL PERDITION

Since it is morals that enable people to live together in harmony and mutual cooperation, the wide acceptance of Gnosticism and its amorality will necessarily lead to the destruction of society. Gnostic pride and sensuality will make of man an *homo homini lupus*, a wolf toward his neighbor, hateful like himself and just as selfish.

Gnostic Mystical Eroticism and the Homosexual Movement

The Gnostic mystical eroticism referred to in *The Da Vinci Code* has much in common with the homosexual movement. We repeat here what we wrote in the book *Defending a Higher Law: Why We Must Resist Same-Sex "Marriage" and the Homosexual Movement.*

> This desire to mix male and female into a new androgynous gender lies at the core of the homosexual ideology. Indeed, the movement's founder Harry Hay starts off his manifesto founding the Mattachine Society with the words, 'We, the androgynes of the world...'[7]
>
> Through the millennia, Gnosis, or Gnosticism, has been the largest wellspring of mystical eroticism. One Gnostic, occultist myth that appears in ancient and current pagan religions claims that in the beginning of Creation there existed a being that was both male and female.... Gnostic mythology claims that man's "redemption" consists in reuniting

---

7. TFP Committee on American Issues, *Defending a Higher Law: Why We Must Resist Same-Sex "Marriage" and the Homosexual Movement* (Spring Grove, Penn.: The American Society for the Defense of Tradition, Family and Property—TFP, 2004), p. 54.

the two sexes and restoring the primeval androgynous being.... The antagonism between the homosexual movement and Christianity is much more
profound than the psychological, scientific, social,
and political arguments so often debated. Harry
Hay, the movement's founder, is clear that the
antagonism is religious. Therefore, it would
appear that the movement's "moral revolution" is
part of an immense effort to supplant Christianity
with a Gnostic, neopagan, erotic mysticism.[8]

---

8.   Ibid., p. 61.

CHAPTER 13
Gnosticism's Attempt to Infiltrate the Church

Gnosticism has long been considered a Christian heresy, for as soon as Christianity began to spread, Gnosticism sought to infiltrate it by adopting Christian concepts and language.

The New Testament and the Church Fathers and Ecclesiastical Writers repeatedly refer to the early Church's difficult struggle against this essentially pagan attempt to hijack Christianity. "This struggle," Fr. Jules Lebreton writes, "was, however, not fruitless; it gave to church authority more vigor, and to dogma greater precision."[1]

SIMON THE MAGICIAN

Already in the Acts of the Apostles we are told that a magician named Simon seduced the people of Samaria, where he was called "the power of God." Later the people and Simon himself converted, being baptized by the Deacon Philip. When the Apostles Peter and John arrived in Samaria to administer the sacrament of Confirmation, Simon, astonished by the prodigies they worked, tried to buy from them what was really a gift of the Holy Spirit.[2]

In his "Magicians Not Trusted By Christians," Saint Justin Martyr writes that this would-be Christian leader was later worshipped as a god in Rome.[3]

GNOSTICS IN THE CHURCH OF CORINTH

In his epistles to the Corinthians, Saint Paul criticizes the presence among them of libertines and blasphemers who pro-

---

1. Lebreton and Zeiller, Vol. 1, p. 359.
2. Acts 8:9–24.
3. Chapter 26 of St. Justin Martyr's *First Apology* (www.newadvent.org/fathers/0126.htm).

nounce an "anathema to Jesus."[4] Such was the practice of the
Gnostic "Christians," who did not accept that Jesus was true
God and true man. Saint John calls these "Christians" liars.[5]
Saint Paul likewise condemns them.

> I give you to understand that no man, speaking by
> the Spirit of God, saith Anathema to Jesus. And no
> man can say The Lord Jesus, but by the Holy Ghost.[6]
> If any man love not our Lord Jesus Christ, let him
> be anathema.[7]

FURTHER CONDEMNATIONS

Other epistles written by the Apostles, the Gospels and the
Apocalypse contain condemnations of the Gnostics.

Saint Jude denounces men who having not the grace of God
infiltrate the Christian community, where they "defile the flesh
and despise dominion and blaspheme majesty."[8]

Saint John fulminates the "Christians" who deny that Christ
is divine and one with the Father. He calls them anti-Christs.[9]
In the Apocalypse he singles out for condemnation the
Nicolaites, Gnostic "Christians" opposed to all moral law. He
says such "Christians" are not true Christians but belong to the
Synagogue of Satan.[10]

Saint Peter warns Christians not to give credence to "artifi-
cial fables" but to accept the Apostles' testimony on the life,
passion, and death of Our Lord Jesus Christ, for "we were eye-
witnesses of his greatness."[11]

---

4. 1 Cor. 12:3.
5. 1 John 2:22. Cf. Walter Schmithals, *Gnosticism in Corinth* (New York: Abingdon Press, 1971), p. 127.
6. 1 Cor. 12:3.
7. 1 Cor. 16:22.
8. Jude 1:4–8.
9. 1 John 2:18–22.
10. Apoc. 2:6, 14–15.
11. 2 Pet. 1:16.

Saint Paul terms the Gnostic prohibitions of marriage and other legitimate practices "doctrines of devils."[12]

Finally, Saint James warns against the "wisdom" that is "earthly, sensual, devilish."[13]

SAINT JOHN REFUTES GNOSTICISM

Saint Jerome, Father and Doctor of the Church (340–420), holds that the Apostle John wrote his Gospel to refute the Gnostics.

> St. John the Evangelist, the last of the Apostles, who Jesus especially loved and who reclined on the Lord's chest, drew out a stream of most pure doctrine so that he was the only one who deserved to hear, at the feet of the Cross, the words "Behold your mother." Already in his time, seeds had been spread all over Asia by heretical Cerinthians[14] and Ebionites[15] and others who denied that Christ had come to the world in his flesh. St. John, who in his epistles called them heretics, was insistently asked by the bishops of Asia and legates of many churches to write about the divinity of the Savior; and for this end, as I will say, to formulate, boldly and adroitly, what the Word of God is. Hence *Ecclesiastical History*[16] narrates that,

---

12. 1 Tim. 4:1–3.
13. James 3:15.
14. "Cerinthus distinguished between Jesus and the Christ, one of the higher aeons, descended upon Jesus, the son of the Demiurge, and afterwards departed from him to return into the Pleroma" (Lebreton and Zeiller, Vol. 2, pp. 620–621, fn. 7).
15. "The doctrines of this sect are said by Irenaeus to be like those of Cerinthus and Carpocrates. They denied the Divinity and the virginal birth of Christ; they clung to the observance of the Jewish Law; they regarded St. Paul as an apostate, and used only a Gospel according to St. Matthew (*Adv. Haer.*, I, xxvi, 2; III, xxi, 2; IV, xxxiii, 4; V, i, 3)" (J. P. Arendzen, s.v. "Ebionites," *The Catholic Encyclopedia*, Vol. 5, p. 243).
16. Written by Eusebius of Caesaria in 325.

pressured by his brothers to write, he responded that write he would if together they would fast to beseech God. As the fasting was over, imbibed with Revelation he uttered the first words coming from heaven: "In the beginning was the Word: and the Word was with God: and the Word was God. The same was in the beginning with God."[17]

NO DEMIURGE CREATED THE WORLD

In the words following those cited by Saint Jerome, Saint John contradicts the Gnostic claims that the Demiurge created the world and that Jesus was not the Word Incarnate.

In the beginning was the Word: and the Word was with God: and the Word was God. The same was in the beginning with God.

All things were made by him: and without him was made nothing that was made. In him was life: and the life was the light of men.

And the light shineth in darkness, and the darkness did not comprehend it.[18]

And the Word was made flesh and dwelt among us (and we saw his glory, the glory as it were of the only begotten of the Father), full of grace and truth.[19]

NO DIVINE SPARK IS NEEDING LIBERATION

Correcting the Gnostic idea that man is divine on account of the "divine spark within," Saint John explains that we can participate in the life of God through supernatural grace, an actual adoption as children of God.

---

17. Cited by Fr. Cornelius à Lapide, *Commentaria in Scripturam Sacram, Comentarius in Evangelium S. Joannis* (Paris: 1881), Vol. 16, p. 288.
18. John 1:1–4.
19. John 1:14.

He was the true light, which enlighteneth every man that cometh into this world. He was in the world: and the world was made by him: and the world knew him not. He came unto his own: and his own received him not. But as many as received him, he gave them power to be made the sons of God, to them that believe in his name. Who are born, not of blood, nor of the will of the flesh, nor of the will of man, but of God.[20]

And of his fullness we all have received.[21]

THE TRUTH AND THE WITNESS BY MARTYRDOM

Attacked doctrinally by Gnostics within, the Church was also persecuted with violence from without. From Our Lord's death on the cross until Constantine's edict of 313 granting freedom to the Church, countless Christians from all walks of life were martyred for holding to the Faith.

The Apostles, with the exception of Saint John, philosophers like Saint Justin, noblewomen like Saint Cecilia, soldiers like those of the Theban Legion, priests, bishops and Popes, all gave their lives for Christ.

And yet the more martyrs there were, the more the Church grew, for as Henri Daniel-Rops states in a study of the early Church, the sublimity of this testimony in blood moves souls.

There is something catching about heroism, to which the human soul, though it may not contain a great deal of nobility, is very susceptible....

Consequently the epic of the martyrs is not merely an episode in time, now over and done with, one definite period of history. It is a fact of unique impor-

---

20. John 1:9–13.
21. John 1:16.

tance lying at the very heart of the Christian faith,
which is bound up with the most essential parts of the
Christian dogmas.[22]

Thus, the early Church prevailed and vanquished
Gnosticism not because of any help from Constantine, but
because of the strength of her divine doctrine and the witness
of her martyrs.

22. Henri Daniel-Rops, *The Church of Apostles and Martyrs* (Garden City, N.Y.:
Image Books, 1962), pp. 248, 253.

Conclusion

As others before us, we have tried in the course of this book to furnish the basic arguments to counter the sophisms and historical errors contained in *The Da Vinci Code*. We hoped to present in a clear and balanced way reasons why we must oppose *The Da Vinci Code*, especially its blasphemous affirmations and the untruths hurled at the Catholic Church.

However, that is not our only goal.

REJECTING *THE DA VINCI CODE* OUTRIGHT

Even if Dan Brown's *The Da Vinci Code* were but a simple work of fiction that did not claim to be based on true facts, scholars, and credible documents, its blasphemous attack on the Catholic faith would still merit our indignant rejection.

These charges and insinuations spur us to reparation and action.

We adore Christ as the God-Man and believe in the One, Holy, Roman, Catholic, and Apostolic Church, the Mystical Body of Christ. Therefore, we reject Dan Brown's blasphemies against our adorable Savior and his historically flawed assertions that Constantine founded the Church and imposed the belief in Christ's divinity.

In seeing our Faith so attacked and our God so offended, we also are offended and feel the duty to rise up in peaceful protest.

A PUBLIC OFFENSE

Our protests take on a special urgency by the fact that *The Da Vinci Code* is not an obscure work of fiction: It is a blockbuster bestseller with over 35 million copies in print worldwide. Hollywood has put its best resources into a film version of the work which will spread its false message far and wide. It is hard to imagine a more widespread promotion of the ideas contained in this book.

Our purpose in writing this book is to fortify the reader against insidious doubts so stealthily introduced on such a grand scale. Most Catholics simply do not have the facts at hand to refute the absurd charges so widely circulated. They need a defense against those who will use the film to question true Catholics about their Faith.

At the same time, it is a public response to a public offense.

Our defense is to affirm what the Catholic Church has always taught for two thousand years, a position as firm as the Rock of Peter. We proudly proclaim that the Church, unlike Her enemies, has no hidden secret or code and has never been afraid to proclaim the truth in its entirety. We challenge the vain and pretentious boast of the film's promoters who claim it will "shake the foundations of Christianity" or "change the course of mankind forever."

A PART OF THE CULTURAL WAR

To grasp completely the gravity of *The Da Vinci Code*'s attack on the Catholic Church, one must go beyond its individual impact.

This is not just a single offensive film. It is part of a wave of blasphemous films, plays, and "art" exhibits that, on one hand, makes Catholics insensitive to the defense of their Faith and, on the other, de-Christianizes America by mocking everything we hold most sacred.

Thus, *The Da Vinci Code* and other such works must be inserted into the context of what political analysts have called a cultural war now being fought between Christianity and militant secularism.

Part of this brutal struggle is found in the efforts to banish God and His Ten Commandments from the public square.

Another major attack is the fashions and media that proclaim ever greater sexual "freedom" from God's moral law in the form of pornography, contraception, adultery, divorce, homosexuality, and now, same-sex "marriage."

However, the wave of blasphemy aims yet further and seeks to wrench the love of God and His Holy Church from our very souls by ridiculing, mocking, and casting doubt on the foundations of our Faith.

We live amid the insecurity of the terrorist threat. If we rightly fear the horrific material damage of these physical attacks, should we not also fear the devastating effect in the spiritual realm caused by this cultural attack that explodes in the depth of our souls, shaking and destroying certainties, principles, and beliefs? Should we not defend ourselves and challenge not just *The Da Vinci Code*, but this whole wave of blasphemies?

THE CODE BEHIND THE CODE

It is ironic that a film that claims to unmask a hidden code would contain its own hidden code.

In unmasking the code behind *The Da Vinci Code*, we hope to dismiss the claims that the book or movie is but mere entertainment.

Mixed in the adrenaline of its fast-paced episodes, one finds a favorable exposition of the tenets of Gnosticism, the devil's false wisdom, with all its mysticism and superstition. Gnosticism offers the doctrinal justification for the despising of all life and, indeed, the entire creation. It is a religion that promotes the perversions of morals. It contradicts Church teachings on every issue.

The Da Vinci Code invites the unsuspecting reader to look

favorably upon this Gnostic vision of God and society. It asks the reader to accept a portrayal that paints the Catholic Church as an enemy of humanity, and presents the devil as a "lame saint."

In face of this hidden code, it is incomprehensible that we simply cross our arms and remain silent.

A GOD REVILED

Finally we invite our readers to look upon this God who is so reviled.

What has this God done to merit such treatment?

Indeed this God has done everything to merit our love, veneration, and adoration. This God became flesh and dwelt amongst us. The marvel of His birth has captivated nations throughout the ages. The richness of His teachings has challenged the greatest intellectuals. His works and miracles were testimony to His desire to come to our aid.

This was a God who took His love for us to a sublime height by offering up His life for our salvation. He was crucified, died and was buried for us. He resurrected from the dead, established His Church, and opened for us the gates of Heaven. From this Church came a glorious Christian civilization.

He did everything for us. He seeks only our well-being. He exhausts no means to call us to salvation.

This book was written to inflame in us a greater love for the adorable Person of Our Lord Jesus Christ. It is only right that we should defend His honor as an act of gratitude and praise. It is only just that we should counter the fantasies of Gnosticism and its anti-church with an increasing fidelity to the Holy Catholic Church founded by Our Lord Jesus Christ. If we do our part, we may be sure that this good God and His Most Holy Mother will come to our aid to carry us to victory.

APPENDIX
Countering the Wave of Blasphemy

TFP–America Needs Fatima has led legal and peaceful public protests against the following blasphemies:

- 1978 – Planned Parenthood's "Abortion Eve." A cartoon of an expectant Blessed Virgin saying, "What me, worry?"
- 1985 – The film *Hail Mary*. A parody of the Annunciation and the Virgin Birth.
- 1988 – The film *The Last Temptation of Christ*. Portrays a Jesus uncertain of His Divinity and fantasizing about married life with Mary Magdalene.
- 1997 – The display of a statue of Our Lady of Grace with a drainpipe through her womb. At the Los Angeles Museum of Contemporary Art.
- 1998 – The play *Corpus Christi*. Includes a Christ-like figure called Joshua who has homosexual relations with his apostles and a long affair with Judas.
- 1999 – The film *Dogma*. The story of a modern-day descendant of Jesus who works in an abortion clinic.
- 1999 – The play *The Most Fabulous Story Ever Told*. Presents the Bible story from a homosexual perspective. Opens with "Adam" and "Steve" expelled from the Garden of Eden and closes with the Blessed Mother portrayed as a lesbian.
- 2000 – The display of a computer collage of a bikini-wearing Virgin of Guadalupe held aloft by a topless female angel. At the Santa Fe Museum of International Folk Art.
- 2001 – The display of photos of a nude woman standing in the place of Jesus at the Last Supper and of a topless woman on a cross. At the Brooklyn Museum of Art.
- 2002 – The play *Jesus Has Two Mommies*. A lesbian

retelling of the Christmas story.

- 2002 – The production of cards by Nobleworks with dirty jokes and cartoons of Jesus, Mary and the Catholic Faith.
- 2002 – The display of defecating figurines of the Pope, a bishop and a nun. At the American Center for Wine, Food and the Arts.
- 2002 – The *Chicago Reader*'s "La Petite Camera, Papal Makeover." A cartoon of the Pope dispensing "red hot birth control pills" and saying, "We were just kidding about Original Sin."
- 2002 – The film *The Crime of Fr. Amaro*. Shows a priest having relations with a 16-year-old girl under the mantle of a statue of Our Lady of Guadalupe, and an alley cat eating a consecrated Host that has been spat on the floor.
- 2003 – The movie *The Magdalene Sisters*. Gives the idea that the Catholic Faith is absurd, its followers sadistic, immoral and unbalanced.
- 2003 – The book *The Da Vinci Code*. With a Gnostic version of the life of Christ. The New Testament is part of the Catholic Church's centuries-long cover-up of the truth.
- 2004 – The sale by Urban Outfitters of "dress-up Jesus" dolls. The dolls can be dressed up with a devil costume, a skull T-shirt, and a hula skirt.

INDEX

The American Society for the Defense of Tradition, Family and Property (TFP) was born of a group of Catholic Americans concerned about the multiple crises shaking every aspect of American life. Founded in 1973, the American TFP was formed to resist, in the realm of ideas, the liberal, socialist and communist trends of the times and proudly affirm the positive values of tradition, family and property. Central to the TFP mission is the idea that the various crises threatening American society and the Catholic Church cannot be seen as separate and disjointed events but rather must be seen as the consequences of a worldwide crisis based on the errors of our times. The TFP handbook *Revolution and Counter-Revolution* by Plinio Corrêa de Oliveira masterfully traces the historical and philosophical roots of the present crisis and proposes a response.

Thus, the TFP is a movement that embraces every field of action, especially in art, ideas and culture. TFP books, publications and newspaper advertisements help bring these views to the public. Moreover, the TFP takes issues to the streets with colorful sidewalk campaigns in major cities.

The first TFP was founded in Brazil in 1960 by Prof. Plinio Corrêa de Oliveira. The American TFP is one of many autonomous TFPs that now exist around the world dedicated to the same ideals and at the service of Christian Civilization. The American TFP's national headquarters is located in Spring Grove, Pennsylvania.

The TFP Committee on American Issues is a study commission recently set up to monitor events in American society and the Church. It issues papers and articles that frequently appear on the TFP website. For more information on the TFP please visit its website at **www.tfp.org**.

Cut out and mail
Book Order Form

Get *Rejecting The Da Vinci Code* today at zero risk and no cost up front!

❑ **YES! Please rush me my copy of *Rejecting The Da Vinci Code* as well as my FREE inspirational picture of the Holy Family. When my book arrives I'll send $10.95 (shipping and handling included.)**

❑ **I'm a college student. (20% discount.)**

Mr./Mrs./Miss_____

Address_____

City_____**St.**_____**Zip**_____

Phone_____**E-mail**_____

Remember, your satisfaction guaranteed with *Rejecting The Da Vinci Code* or your money back. Either way, you get a FREE picture of the Holy Family.

Please detach, complete, fold and return this form to TFP .

Tradition, Family, Property (TFP)
P.O. Box 251
Spring Grove, PA 17362

Toll free 1-866-661-0272 • www.tfp.org

Revolution and Counter-Revolution

by *Plinio Corrêa de Oliveira*

If anything characterizes our times, it is a sense of pervading chaos. In every field of human endeavor, the windstorms of change are fast altering the ways we live. Contemporary man is no longer anchored in certainties and thus has lost sight of who he is, where he comes from and where he is going. If there is a single book that can shed light amid the postmodern darkness, this is it.

180 pages, paperback, © 2003. **$9.95**

I Have Weathered Other Storms

A Response to the Scandals and Democratic Reforms that Threaten the Catholic Church

by *TFP Committee on American Issues*

Powerfully documented, fully indexed and richly illustrated, this 180-page book delves into the profound crisis of Faith, media blitz and bias, and a reformists' agenda for changing the Church.

This book put the crisis in a much-needed supernatural perspective. The Church is not just any organization; it has indeed weathered other storms.

First Edition, 192 pages, paperback, © 2002. **$12.95**

Defending a Higher Law

Why We Must Resist Same-Sex "Marriage"and the Homosexual Movement

by *TFP Committee on American Issues*

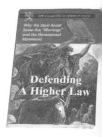

This 212-page book is a much needed defense of traditional marriage based on Catholic tradition and natural law. It is a powerful and incisive attack on the myths buttressing homosexual agenda.

First Edition, 212 pages, paperback, © 2003. **$12.95**